Prayer:
CLOSET POWER

Nelson L. Price

Prayer: Closet Power

Copyright © 2007 by Nelson L. Price

Published by
Nelson Price Ministries, Inc.
1400 Beaumont Drive
Kennesaw, GA 30152
www.nelsonprice.com

Library of Congress Catalog-in-Publication Data
Price, Nelson L.
Prayer: Closet Power
ISBN-13: 978-0-9794754-1-2
1. Inspiration
2. Religion: Christianity
1. Title

To the Prayer Warriors whose intercession
on my behalf has enriched my life----
especially my constant companion,
Trudy, and our beloved extended family.
Nelson L. Price

CONTENTS

INTRODUCTION

The pastor's study in the First Baptist Church of Washington D.C. was my prayer closet on this memorable morning. The thirty-ninth President of the United States was about to be Inaugurated. He had asked that I preach at his Inaugural Worship Service two hours before he took the oath of office. I was in the office alone praying when the father-in-law of the Vice President entered and apologized for the disturbance saying, "I see you are doing what our Quaker friends call 'centering down.'"

That is a distilled definition of prayer. It is admitting God into our heart's inner court yard there to be enthroned.

The following statement taken for the "Society of Friends' Queries" amplifies this concept.

"Do you make a place in your daily life for inward retirement and waiting upon God, that you may learn the full meaning of prayer and the joy of communion with Him? And do you live in daily dependence upon His help and guidance?"

Such a retreat center where you meet alone with God is a place to report for duty and be re-supplied for life..

Prayer is to life what a global positioning satellite (GPS) is to a traveler. It lets you know where you are and how to get to where you need to go. Keep it turned on, pray without ceasing.

May this work inspire you to go to your "prayer closet" and center down!

1
YOU ARE NOT IN THE DARK
IN THE CLOSET

Entering the small closet under the steps in this quaint Old Southern home I realized I was on holy ground. This stately home in Oxford, Mississippi, had served as a base from which our Lord directed productive ministries. Mrs. Corra Belly Leavell retreated to this small chamber with regularity to pray for her nine sons. Her pure heart beat in cadence with the Heavenly Heartbeat.

Daily she systematically called the name of each of them in the ear of her Heavenly Father with urgency. By her prayers that quaint little mother was to sweeten the stream of life. One of her nine became a dentist and served the Lord in Hollywood, California. The other eight became pastors, missionaries, or denominational workers. The three subsequent generations have also produced children of strong Christian convictions. Many of them also serve in church-related ministries. One grandson, Landrum Leavell III, has four children all of which are in Christian ministries.

There is power in the closet!

The closet is to the Christian world what the mechanical

room is to a building. It is the point of origin for all energy sources.

In the vernacular of the Bible, "the closet" is private prayer. Strange, isn't it, that in the secular world "the closet" is usually a reference to secret sin. To the worldly-oriented person the vogue thing is to "come out of the closet." Conversely, the only way to counter the tidal wave pouring out of the carnal closet is for the Christian to "enter into his closet and pray."

The secret of praying is praying in secret.

Pointed, private prayer is one of the best ways to allow the Lord to prove Himself. When only the person praying and the Lord know of the prayer, all human manipulation is prevented. By that I mean indirect begging is avoided. Some persons have mastered the art of soliciting from persons by appearing to entreat the Lord in public prayer. An even more direct way of making a subtle request is to tell persons "I am praying God will give me ..." Skillfully done this sets up a friend to do what God may or may not want done simply because it sounds spiritual.

Bill entered his closet with purpose. Bill isn't his real name, but I have chosen it as a pseudonym to fully protect the "closet" nature of this experience.

Bill was in full-time ministry. He served the Lord on the national staff of a splendid para-church organization. In preparation for service he had engaged in extensive Bible study. He had followed his good friend, alias Rocky, as college quarterback. Rocky had enjoyed a prestigious pro career.

Bill needed transportation badly. He entered his "closet" and prayed, "Lord, I think I need a car, any car. I think I need transportation to serve you better. If you agree with me, please provide it. There is no way I can afford a car. You own the cars on a thousand sales lots. I want what you want and only what you want. If you want me to have a car, please provide it."

Rocky was just finishing one of his story-book years in the NFL and getting ready for the Super Bowl. He was at the time a Biblically illiterate Christian. Church groups were appealing to him to speak at the conclusion of the season. He called Bill and explained his lack of Bible knowledge and sought his help. They agreed that every night Rocky would call Bill and Bill would give him a short course, a Bible overview, by phone. This they did for a month. The conversations often lasted so long, it ended almost as a post grad course.

The Super Bowl ended with Rocky being named MVP. Soon thereafter he called Bill. The essence of the conversation was, "Bill, could you use a car? I received a new one for being named NFL Player of the Year and a second one for being Super Bowl MVP. I can't use two new cars, and I thought perhaps you could use one."

Bill had not hinted to Rocky of his need of a car. No mention had been made regarding his prayers for one. Therefore, when Rocky gave Bill the car, he was simply serving as the Lord's delivery boy. God supplied the car through Rocky in answer to Bill's prayer. That's closet power.

Such prayer with the door "shut" gives the Lord a rare opportunity. It is not required that all prayer be private. It is, however, one form commended by our Lord. A "shut door" is an open opportunity for the Lord.

A friend stopped to make a phone call in a public booth. It being dark he searched for a means to turn on the light in the booth. A companion said, "The light goes on when you shut the door." Prayer closets are like phone booths. Shut the door and the light goes on.

WHAT IS A CLOSET?

Jesus said, "But thou, when thou prayest, enter into thy closet, and when thou has shut the door, pray to thy Father which is in secret; and thy Father which seeth in secret shall reward thee openly" (Matthew 6:6).

The Greek text used the word TAMEION which can be translated "closet," "inner room," "storeroom," or simply "room." Originally it was used as a storeroom in which valuables were locked. Prayer is thus depicted as being the treasure it really is. As used here it isn't a reference to a literal place, but rather to privacy. This privacy can be achieved by an actual room. As an encouragement to pray it is good to have a place specially designated for prayer. You know what it is for when you go there. Consequently, it is an encouragement to prayer.

Some years ago I had lunch on board the flagship for the Atlantic Fleet with the Captain. After the meal he took me on an insightful tour of the ship. Deep in the belly of the ship we entered a white room. Upon shutting the door the Captain asked, "What do you hear?" I listened attentively supposing there to be something I should hear. Strain as I might I finally had to confess I couldn't hear anything. With a smile he said, "This room is completely insulated to close out all sounds. It is the control center for the fleet. No matter what happens in the heat of combat no sound will disturb us in here. Without distractions we can think and plan better."

That room was arranged and designated for a specific use. It was conducive for its intended purpose. If at all possible, every believer needs a "control central." Establish one if possible. It can be small and simple. In it should be your Bible, any devotional book you might prefer, and two comfortable places; one for sitting and one for kneeling. It might be as commendable as a special room in your home. It might be as simple as your bed side.

Sitting on the pinnacle of the roof of the 4,000 seat Roswell Street Baptist Church in Marietta, Georgia, is a prayer tower. It stands nine stories above the ground with a commanding view of all around it. When the building plans were being reviewed for approval, it was said such a room could not be approved as a prayer tower. Almost parenthetically the inspector said it could be approved if it were an observation tower. "An observation tower," I exclaimed, "that is what it is. You can see all the way to heaven from there." After all, Isaac Newton said, "I can take my telescope and look millions of miles into space; but I can lay my telescope aside, get down on my knees in earnest prayer, and I can see more of heaven and get closer to God than I can when assisted by all the telescopes and material agencies on earth." The "observation tower" was approved and has proven to be a wonderful place to pray.

Whether it is possible to designate an area for prayer or not, the purpose can and should always be achieved every time we pray. "Entering into your closet", even when you are in public, means to shut out all things going on around you and centering in on the presence of the Lord. Exclude all else and concentrate on confronting Him. Closet-praying is the art of being alone with the Lord even if being televised from a stadium filled to capacity. It is being conscious of God alone. Being in His presence takes supersedence over all else. A preoccupation with Who is being addressed excludes any consciousness of where you are or who you are with. This is true relational prayer. It is you alone relating to God only.

CLOSET PRAYING DOESN'T ABOLISH PUBLIC PRAYER

Many things blend together to make for a good prayer life. Unfortunately some persons find only one Scriptural requirement and stress it to the omission of all others. Some say all that is necessary for a good prayer life is for "two or three" to "agree." That is one very good point, but only one. There are many. A few examples of the several that will be stressed in this book are: spiritual cleansing, obedience to the Word, a yielded life, requesting that which is within the will of the Lord, and persistence. All of these need to be combined for there to be a good prayer life.

At this point it needs to be made clear this is not a teaching against prayer in public places. This text is a prohibition against ostentatious or showy prayers.

Jesus prayed in public. At the grave of Lazarus He prayed publicly in order that the Father might be glorified in answering the prayer (John 11: 41 - 43). The hallmark of this prayer should be the reason for all prayer: "that they might believe..." Jesus prayed it publicly as a confirmation of His deity.

Prudent public prayer in the temple was used by Jesus to expose inappropriate public display, and commend proper public prayer (Luke 18: 6 - 14). Jesus depicted a publican praying with a humble heart and contrite spirit. This He commended. He depicted a Pharisee arrogantly praying with an air of superiority. His self-embellishment which took the form of a prayer was offensive to our Lord. Again the issue is stressed as not being where but how we pray. The submitted publican though viewed as in public was mentally and spiritually in his "closet."

Some years ago while traveling in Brazil a saintly missionary, Rasalee Mills Appleby, gave me a book inscribed, "One can't expect to count for God who isn't long alone with Him." Hers was an appeal for piety growing out of familiarity with God. Such requires much closet time. It is amazing how much better known He becomes when encountered in the closet.

A WARNING AGAINST PLAY-ACTING

Jesus termed persons who prayed like the Pharisee "hypocrites," HYPOKRITES. The term in Greek referred to a role-player. Actors in legitimate theaters were called "hypokrites." In the theater the same actor or actress might play several roles.

To achieve this costumes were changed, different masks employed, and various vocal inflections used. Those to whom Jesus referred used the street corner and temple as their stage.

Hypocrisy is a tribute to dishonesty.

Hypocrites come in three basic stripes. One knows he or she is deceptive. Though evil and aware of it, this person designs ways of deceiving; that is, looking righteous. A second, more advanced form of hypocrisy, results in the "actor" even deceiving himself or herself. This person can change roles and persuade self of genuineness in either. In advanced cases this person becomes a split personality. Thus, both roles are false. A third classification of hypocrite is even more acute. These persons convince themselves their role-play is best for God and mankind. These persons have played the roles so long they have convinced and deceived themselves. Some such persons occasionally emerge in leadership roles in the Christian community before being exposed. Such a person is a decoy of Satan; a bait for disbelief.

Exposure of such a one is always discouraging, but it should not cause despair. Remember, there was one among Christ's twelve apostles. They existed in the emerging young church of the New Testament. Such conduct was wrong then and is now. The day inevitably comes when "...the hypocrite's hope shall perish" (Job 8: 13b).

Jesus was adamantly opposed to hypocrisy. In addition to His denunciation of play-acting in prayer, He also censured persons giving in a flamboyant manner. He warned givers "do not sound the trumpet" when giving. There is no record of trumpets being used in the temple in conjunction with giving. However, the funnel like opening into which offerings were placed was somewhat trumpet shaped. Evidently some persons had learned just how to throw their large coin when giving so that it would circle around the edge going down and make the maximum noise. This method of calling attention to oneself was called "sounding the trumpet." Jesus appealed to persons to give as well as to pray in an unhypocritical manner.

Jesus warned, "And when thou prayest, thou shalt not be as the hypocrites are..." (Matthew 6: 5). A personal warning sign of play-acting is available. A person who prays more in public than in private should read his or her own spiritual pulse. Such inversion of priorities reveals a person is more interested in public accolades than God's approval.

It is the public announcement technique which often constitutes indirect begging that is condemned. Any alleged prayer that is offered to solicit goods from a person to gain compliments for self, to make a proclamation, or give glory to any but the Lord is inappropriate.

PRAYER IS RELATIONAL

In the statement of prayer recorded by Matthew, Jesus is teaching us prayer is relational. It is a personal relationship between God and man, not man and man. Through prayer we expose ourselves to God and make ourselves vulnerable to His will. It is being "honest to God."

In a heartfelt prayer there is always a white flag waving over the headquarters of your heart. It is an invitation to the Lord to occupy control central of your life.

Don't try to impress God with your prayer. Let Him impress you as a result of you praying. It is humbling to think that our sovereign God has chosen not to superimpose His will on us. He, therefore, waits for us to yield our will to Him before He will act. It is not that we finally convince God of our viewpoint, but rather that He finally converts us to His will; and we happily say, "OK, God I now want your will even more than I want mine." He already knows what is best for us and has just been waiting for us to say "I am ready to receive it." At this point supernatural things begin to happen. Once we recognize Him and relent to His will, the relationship has been forged. He is then free to function in our lives in accordance to the extent of our willful surrender.

This relationship with the Lord, through prayer, results in the person praying being conformed to the image of Christ. That image is proportionate to the time and heartfelt nature of the prayer. Both time and heart are essentials. It takes time to be still and know God. Time is required to wait on the Lord, but "They that wait upon the Lord shall renew their strength; they shall mount up with wings as eagles; they shall run, and not be weary; and they shall walk, and not faint" (Isaiah 40:31). Jeremiah penned this promise from God Himself: "Ye shall seek me, and find me, when ye shall search for me with all your heart" (Jeremiah 29:13). Half-hearted prayer is fully unproductive.

Time invested in heartfelt prayer results in a supernatural transformation. "But we all, with open face beholding, as in a glass the glory of the Lord, are changed into the same image from glory to glory, even by the Spirit of the Lord" (II Corinthians 3:18). Ideally, prayer makes us mirror reflections of Christ.

Few people are called to a ministry of prayer like John Welch, the son-in-law of the Scotch reformer John Knox. It was Welch not Knox who prayed, "Give me Scotland or I die." Shortly before his death, Welch shared with friends that any day he did not pray seven or eight hours he considered not well spent. Upon the death of John Welch an old Scotchman who had known him for years remarked, "John Welch was a type of Christ." Though some might argue with the language of this comment all would have to consent the result was admirable. Welch was like a negative in a dark room on which the image of Christ was developed. Time spent in heartfelt prayers left that image on him as it will on any person.

CLOSET PRAYER IS COSTLY

The discipline required for closet prayer is demanding. There simply isn't any time in a busy modern schedule for prayer. You can't take time for prayer -- you must make time for it. Discipline begets discipline. A life undisciplined in other regards will find it difficult to spend time in prayer. Spending time in prayer will develop other disciplines and aid all.

Mark Twain said, "Life is a limitless multiplication of unnecessary necessities." Amen! The key to a vital time of prayer is subtracting those expendables on your schedule and rightly dividing your time. You can add to your spiritual vitality by doing so. To make time for prayer something must be given up. Review your schedule and see what can best go. Perhaps it is a bit of sleep. By setting your clock a little earlier you might provide the time needed. Early morning prayer helps get a day off to a good start. Some persons find it advantageous to pick a day each week and reserve the noon meal-time for prayer. By skipping the meal this can be a form of fasting and praying. Use your imagination and will to designate regular times of prayer.

Perhaps Christians are the least disciplined in prayer of all religions. Seven times a day Muslims pray. They even get up during the night to pray. Cultural habits mark extended times of prayer among some religious groups. Though they might be driven by fear, habit, or custom; they do it. We being motivated by love and blessings should be even more highly motivated to pray.

Jesus taught this lesson in a demonstrative culture. The Pharisees of His day loved to parade their piety. Their style of praying was contrary to the will of God. For them public prayers had become clinics on style, speech, and superficial spirituality. Such formal prayers were used by them to exhibit their hypocritical religion. They wanted to overwhelm people, not surrender to the Lord. Jesus said they got what they wanted; the praise of people. When Jesus said "they have their reward" He meant they have been "paid in full;" that's all they are going to get. Unfortunately their pretense availed little with the Lord. Well, after all that wasn't what they wanted anyway.

"You know, I couldn't hear a word of Peabody's prayer," said Dr. Charles W. Eliot of Harvard, after the celebration of his ninetieth birthday. Smiling back at him his wife said, "He wasn't speaking to you, dear!"

We too must keep in mind the One to whom we are speaking and speak only to Him.

In our quiet time alone with God in the closet He who has no need of utterance speaks in an inaudible voice most clear.

When the door of your closet, be it literal or figurative, closes you will find the Lord there waiting for you. The imagination is stretched by His invitation: "Call unto me, and I will answer thee, and shew thee great and mighty things, which thou knowest not" (Jeremiah 33:3). Now that you know God's phone number, call Him frequently, toll free, thanks to Jesus.

2
QUALIFICATIONS AND QUALITIES OF PRAYER

Jeanne greeted me with a smile as I entered her hospital room. Her refreshing beauty and characteristic radiance had been eroded by cancer. For days her excruciating physical pain had been made more agonizing by the emotion of her plight. Faintly but enthusiastically she spoke, "Pastor, I am ready for God to heal me..." In that momentary pause I thought anyone would be ready for that. She resumed, "I am ready for God to heal me...to take me home...or...." After pausing she concluded, "or let me suffer like this in His name."

To this day that constitutes one of the most beautiful "Thy will be done" prayers I have heard. Her response to her suffering, which lasted a few more weeks, was glorifying to our Lord. Her faithfulness unto death was a testimony of God's sustaining grace.

In less extenuating, non-life-threatening circumstances, are you ready to pray such a prayer? She, like our Lord, by example taught us of the victory in such submissiveness. Unconditional surrender guarantees uncompromising victory.

The best thing that happened to Japan in World War II was her unconditional surrender to the United States. When the surrender was completed and the war ended, an unprecedented change happened in Japan. America then undertook the reconstruction of the war-depleted nation. Once Japan surrendered then the attributes and assets of America became hers. The very force against which she had struggled now became her source of strength. Upon the cessation of hostility, her adversary became her ally.

Application of that principle to our own spiritual lives is obvious. The uncompromising surrender inherent in the Gethsemane proviso opens the door for the Lord to place at our disposal His resources. For relinquishing our obstinacy we lose nothing and gain heavenly help.

Consider now some qualifications and qualities of proper prayer.

QUALIFICATIONS
Qualification Number One

"The effectual fervent prayer of a righteous man availeth much" (James 5:16). As most persons read that verse interest rises toward the end. The last two words "availeth much" makes it appealing to many. It seems to be a formula for getting what you want. That excites most. A closer look at the full text reveals a truth even more exciting.

The conscientiousness of the person praying. There are two different Greek words for "prayer." PROSEUCHE is the word used for prayer in general. The one used here, DEESIS, puts emphasis on a specific need, conveying a sense of urgency and importance. It carries the idea of fervent earnestness and intensity. Anything important enough to take up God's time ought to be done with zeal.

The character of the pray-er. For prayer to be effective it must be offered by a "righteous" person. "Righteousness," DIKAIOU, is used in a moral sense meaning the Christians' quality of life. It refers to a lifestyle pleasing to the Lord. Roses don't grow in rock gardens, and prayers don't blossom in lives where there is habitual sin.

The consequence of the prayer. A fervent prayer offered by a righteous person will be "effectual." A careful review of this truth reveals that the primary productivity of such a prayer is internal not external. This is a word used to speak of the working of God. Thus, such a pray-er is bringing God into the formula. By using the present participle form, reference is made to "its in working"; that is, it is internal in its effect in the life of the person praying. Such a prayer really impacts that life. Inherent in the act is the blessing. Any answer is simply an added benefit. Such a prayer is a means God has chosen to bring about His divine will.

Qualification Number Two

Jesus said "pray ye, our Father..." (Matthew 6:9). Jesus thus gave believers direct access to the Father. No intermediary is needed. A preoccupation with the One being addressed is expedient in prayer. Concentrate on the One being addressed more than on that for which you are praying.

Disturbing misunderstanding exists regarding this aspect of prayer. This was dramatized in a hospital room in New Orleans. All afternoon and into the night I had kept an anxious vigil with loving parents whose ten year-old daughter hovered on the brink of death. Several times we had specific prayer. On occasion we prayed with and for the attending doctor as he came out to bring reports. Then came the grievous moment. As the doctor came out of the emergency room, his facial expression indicated what he confirmed: "I regret to tell you your child has just died." A child beautiful in body and spirit had gone to be with the only One who loved her more than her parents. After moments of consolation, the doctor returned and pulled me aside. "I know you folks have prayed for this child," he said, "but please tell her parents they no longer need to pray for her. They can now pray to her. She's a saint." This typifies a common false belief. Not only is intercession by a saint not necessary, it is not allowed.

Thank God no intermediary is needed. We have direct access to the Father. God is never too busy to hear from you. The problem related to time in prayer is always on this end of the line.

Qualification Number Three

"For ye have not received the spirit of bondage again to fear; but ye have received the Spirit of adoption, whereby we cry, 'Abba, Father'" (Romans 8:15).

In Roman culture adoption put a person in relation of son to a father. Under their law even slaves could be adopted as sons. A ceremony performed in the presence of witnesses resulted in a new relationship, privileges, and responsibilities. During the ritual, the adopting father paid all debts against the adoptee. The adopted child became a joint heir with natural-born children. He was esteemed as having been "born again" into a new family.

The Greek word for father, PATER, speaks of relationship and understanding. The Aramaic, ABBA, reveals trust, obedient surrender, and unconditional faith. It was everyday language used by little helpless children addressing their dad.

To address God as Father means we would not dare knowingly ask Him for anything contrary to His will. We should rather seek wholeheartedly to think, say, and do what pleases Him. As a loving and obedient child delights to please his earthly father, great pleasure is derived from pleasing our Heavenly Father.

Where there is a good father/child relationship, the child desires and delights in pleasing the parent. An attitude of loving dependance and trust exists. Like a little child performing for his Dad calling out, "Watch me, Dad, watch me," so we should desire to be open before and pleasing to our heavenly Father. Approval by the Father is all the child wants. Therein is our greatest gratification in prayer also.

Qualification Number Four
"And whatsoever ye shall ask in my name, that will I do, that the Father may be glorified in the Son" (John 14:13).

In giving the authority to pray in His name Jesus instructs us to pray as His proxy, in His stead. This means that when we pray, we pray as we believe Christ would pray if in our place under existing circumstances. Such prayer is offered as Christ's alter ego or "other self." This concept is intended to and should make us stop and carefully word our prayers.

To pray in His name means more than merely annexing a formula on the end of a prayer: "For this we ask in Jesus' name." Don't try to offer an unworthy or offensive present before the throne of God in this beautiful wrapping. We should use the phrase "in Jesus' name," but it does not assure that it actually is in Jesus' name. Is it really what Jesus would ask for? If it is in Jesus' name, it is within the Father's will.

To pray truly in Christ's name is to pray as His vicar. Vicar means "instead of." The word is misapplied in some religious circles, but it has relevance here. It comes from the Latin word vicarious. The title "vice-president" holds the meaning. If a president dies, the vice-president becomes the president "instead of" the president who died.

When we pray in His name we pray as one with Christ whose desires are His desires, whose purpose is His purpose. We should never ask for anything that would violate His will or imply we want Him to contradict Himself to provide our desire.

Christ is no longer bodily here on earth. We, as His representatives, have opportunity to represent Him before the throne of the Father in prayer. To do so is to pray truly in His name. Make certain that what is contained between "Our Father..." and "in the name of Jesus Christ" is within the will of the Father. That allows no room for pride, selfishness, or an unforgiving spirit.

Qualification Number Five

"If you love Me, keep My commandments" (John 14:15). Jesus tied making our prayer request in His name closely to obedience. No fervent prayer can come from a disrespectful and disobedient person. Lips that say "Thy will be done" must be supported by a life of obedience. A lack of obedience evidences obstinacy to God's will.

Jesus noted a simple test to determine our love. He said, "If anyone loves Me, he will keep My word..." (John 14:23). He then played the flip side, "He who does not love Me does not keep My words..." (John 14:24).

Consequently, it is self-evident that the person who loves Jesus keeps His commandments, and the person who doesn't keep His commandments doesn't love Him.

To make the test even more forceful Christ used the emphatic pronoun "He." This meant "He and he alone is the one that loves me." Love is the spring of action. It is known by the action it prompts. A parent doesn't tell a child to clean his room simply because he wants the child to know the room is dirty. The parent wants action. Christ does not tell us to do a thing simply because He wants us to know it needs to be done, but because He wants action.

A friend shared with me the following expanded translation which is in reality a commentary of Christ's comment. "If with love that is both intellectual and purposeful you love Me, you will accept, obey, and stand guard over the rules which I have laid down for the regulation of your inner attitudes and outer conduct."

All persons are prompted to pray when there is a crisis. No person can tell in advance when a crisis is going to happen. Therefore, it is impossible to know when an effective prayer life is going to be needed. Waiting until there is a need in order to get ready to meet that need is not wise. To have a good, clear channel for prayer at all times, it is essential to live in obedience to the will of the Father. Out of such a lifestyle can come effective prayer in an instance.

Qualification Number Six

"Pray without ceasing" (I Thess. 5:17) is Paul's command to Christians. "How is that possible?" comes the retort. No matter how devout and desirous a person might be it is self evident that no one can remain in an uninterrupted state of prayer. If that is true, what then does the statement mean?

The word translated "without ceasing" is ADIALEIPTOS. Help in understanding a word is gained by observing how it was used at the time of origin. In the era of the New Testament the word was used in secular writings to describe a person who had a cough. Regardless of how serious the cough might have been, it was not one long, drawn-out, unending cough. The cough would be intermittent coughs at intervals. At a given instance the person might not be coughing, but he still had the cough. Therefore, it could not be said the person had stopped coughing. Likewise, though we may not at a given moment be engaged in prayer, that doesn't mean we have stopped praying.

Disobedience to this principle involved two of my friends. One, a former professor at a seminary left the ministry and joined the social science faculty at LSU. Knowing of his colleague's background, the head of the department privately asked if he would pray at the forthcoming retirement dinner for a fellow professor. Haughtily the former theologian answered, "I will not. I no longer believe in that sort of thing." This person had "ceased" praying--he no longer did it.

Closer intervals of conscious prayer make for a better prayer life. However, the intervals between stopping and starting don't mean a person has ceased praying. Such a person abides in a prayer mood and can pick up where he left off at any moment.

A pilot remains in communication with the control tower even if he is not speaking over the airwaves. Having established contact, the frequency remains open for renewed interchange at any moment. He is thus in constant communication at all times though not actually articulating. Even when we are not engaged in prayer, we can abide in a state of prayer by maintaining an openness to the Lord. A state of prayer makes you so intimate with the Lord that you hardly have an experience before talking to Him about it. This may involve one or more of several qualities.

QUALITIES

A glossary of prayer types should include:

* Adoration -- worship of God.
* Confession -- admission of sin.
* Petition -- requests regarding personal needs.
* Intercession -- intervention on behalf of another.
* Thanksgiving -- heartfelt expression of joy.
* Praise -- a celebration of God's nature and works.

The Psalmist offered us this good pattern for praying: "Evening, and morning, and at noon, will I pray..." (Psalms 55: 17).

As a suggestion, morning is a grand time for adoration,

worship, and confession. Noon is a fitting time for petition and intercession. Evening should evoke thanksgiving and praise. Often these aspects of prayer are interwoven. It is not necessary to separate them, nor is it essential that every prayer include all of them. Overall, one's prayer life should include each.

Adoration. Worship of the Lord is perhaps the most over-looked aspect of prayer. Even our assemblies, which we call "worship", often become anything but worship. To better understand true worship, we find the word for it is traceable to the Greek word for "dog." Dog owners or casual observers of the relationship between a dog and its master can understand this correlation. The well cared for dog responds to its loving master energetically. When the dog comes into his master's presence he comes alive. There is an animation that evidences itself with glowing eyes, wagging tail, panting, and wiggling. These are ways a dog has of expressing adoration, admiration, veneration, love, esteem, awe, and respect. Crude as it may sound, to worship means "to do the dog to." Our joy over coming into the presence of the Lord should manifest itself by our exuberant response. Worship is therapeutic for the worshipper. It brings out the best qualities in each of us. It is a time when the ingredients of life are balanced. Resultantly, we flush ego-tism, abandon vanity, forsake snobbery, and desert boastful-ness. Happily we humble ourselves under the mighty hand of God that He might, at the time of His choosing, exalt us.

Worship puts things in perspective. For example, in look-ing at Goliath many may have said, "Look how small David is compared to Goliath." With eyes of faith others may have seen it differently and said, "Look how small Goliath is compared to David's God." Problems pale when compared with the One to Whom we look for solutions. Worship reminds us of the values the world tends to make us forget.

In worship we are carried far enough from the close-ups

of life to enable us to see our horizons, to re-orient ourselves, and re-chart our direction. Worship frees us from ourselves. We should desire this liberation in light of the fact we are poor masters. Made to be good servants we will never be good self-masters. To worship means to put God in His proper place in our life. When we do our life becomes balanced. In true worship, whether public or private, we enter into the vestibule of God's presence to establish, maintain, and grow in our relationship with Him.

It is dangerously easy to be betrayed by our deceptive conscience. Having been schooled in the world's fine art of rationalization, we can reason our way through most moral mazes. We have become artists at self-delusion. Worship makes a frontal assault on such self-exoneration. It lets us sense the holiness of God and the sinfulness of sin. By it we are prompted to aspire to the former and be repelled by the latter.

Confession. Most of us have more to confess than we are prone to admit. An evangelist appealed to a man to repent and confess his sins. The fellow answered, "I don't know what I should confess." The evangelist encouraged him by saying, "Well, just get on your knees and guess." He concluded by saying, "Would you believe it, he guessed right the first time."

John reminds us of one reason confession is essential: "Now we know that God heareth not sinners..." (John 9:31). Habitual sin restricts prayer and inhibits the sinner. Confession is essential to clear the line of communication. Sin is a repression to our relationship to the Lord. The Lord wants us to take care of first things first. Our relationship with Him must come first. Therefore, before moving on to petition or praise, pause and seek pardon. When we, like the prophet Isaiah, recognize the holiness of God we realize our sinfulness and want cleansing. Worship will automatically be followed by confession. It wasn't until "David's heart smote him" that he said, "I have sinned greatly in that I have done." Only when the prodigal son "came to himself" did he acknowledge "I have sinned."

The word "confess" comes from the Greek ECH-HOMO-LOGO which means "out of the same word." It means to agree with God about sin and call it what God would call it. Therefore, to confess is to express outwardly what the Holy Spirit has shown you inwardly about sin.

Confession is spiritual house cleaning.

Not only does unconfessed sin clog the prayer channel, it curtails our progress. Ageless wisdom is found in Proverbs 28: 13: "He that covereth his sins shall not prosper: but whosoever confesseth and forsaketh them shall have mercy." In this text God has set before us clear alternatives. One is our covered pet sin. The other is our prosperity predicated on His mercy. The options are His mercy or our misery. It is strange that we often have difficulty making such an obvious choice. Like college freshmen trying to deceive a hall monitor who has the experience of the ages, we still try to fool God. Our daring willingness to confess is an admission to God that we prefer His grace to our own "fig-leaves."

"The highest moment in a man's career," wrote Oscar Wilde while in jail for his own law violation, "may be the moment when he kneels in the dust and beats upon his breast and tells all the sins of his life."

Abraham Lincoln found these words for his devotional book most gratifying:

"Ah! Whither could we flee for aid
When tempted, desolate, dismay'd;
Or how the hosts of hell defeat,
Had suffering saints no mercy seat."
From "Lincoln's Devotional"

Petition. Most of us need little encouragement in this aspect of prayer. Perhaps as much as 90 percent of our prayer time is devoted to petitioning God on our own behalf. Many wait to pray until there is a need. Crisis cultivates prayer.

It is alright for a child to give his or her Dad a "Christmas list" of things desired. However, if that were the only communication between them, it would reveal an unhealthy relationship. It is proper for us to let the Lord know of our needs. He has told us to "ask, seek, and knock." The initial letters of these three words spell ASK.

For reasons that defy our logic, God has chosen to set limits on Himself. He has chosen prayer as a means by which to gauge our readiness for His blessings. Andrew Murray has written that "God's will needs prayer as its indispensable condition." Our prayers make a difference in what God is willing to entrust to us. The Holy Spirit solicits from our hearts the prayers necessary for God's will to be done in our lives.

Prayers of petition help us set our priorities. When prone to pray for a certain thing we are given reason to ask, "Is this really what the Lord wants?" Such honest inquiry inevitably results in us removing certain items from our ASK list. When looked at through Bible bifocals, some things are seen to be out of focus with God's will even before requested. That is one of the blessings of prayer. It often changes our minds to conform to the mind of the Father. That in itself is enough to motivate us to pray. This alignment of wills always puts us on the right path.

To ask of the Lord is to admit to Him dependence and trust. It is to let Him know you want the final check-off to be made by Him. By incorporating Him in your plans, you can be confident when the petition is granted. If what you ask is according to His will, you can be assured that in the moment of the asking "we have the petitions that we desire of Him" (I John 5:15). When He is allowed to be our Master, He then is more than simply our Divine Quartermaster, though He is that. Everything He issues "fits."

Asking puts your desires under His will. You are then in a no-lose position. If you are granted the petition, it will be good for you. If you don't get it, that too will be good for you.

Intercession. "I exhort therefore, that,...intercessions...be made for all men" (II Timothy 2:1). Intercession is, therefore, legitimized by the Lord. It is a needful part of prayer. In the other forms of prayer two people are involved--the one praying and the One to which the prayer is offered. Now a third is introduced, the person for which you pray. Here is where love steps outside a "me-tight" world and enters vicariously into the life of another.

God won't make any one of us do His will. Therefore, to try to force someone through prayer to act contrary to his or her own will is folly. Intercessory prayer is not like a supernatural rope thrown over the rafters of heaven and lowered to be attached to another person whereby to manipulate that person. If what we are praying about involves the will of another, the best we can pray is, "Dear God, please bring increasing influences on this person to give an even greater occasion to know and do your will."

I was given a never-to-be-forgotten lesson in intercessory prayer by a small group of athletes. I had just spoken to the entire team and was about to leave when approached by one of them. "A few of us always get together about this time on game days and have a prayer meeting. Would you please join us?" We gathered in a small circle and at their instruction we began to pray around the room. They tutored me in intercession even as it relates to opponents. Each young athlete, in essence, prayed asking the Lord to bless them and help them play up to their potential. Not one asked for a victory. Their youthful innocence seemed to sense God may not even like football though He loves football players. Then came the revealing part of their prayers. They interceded for their opponents by asking the Lord to "help each player on that other team play his best." That revealed to me that intercessory prayer growing out of love desires for our opponents what we desire for ourselves-- the best possible. If you don't clearly know what is best, evidence to God you contentedly leave the choice to Him.

To say to a person "I'm praying for you," is another way of saying "I love you." There is no more meaningful way to communicate love than to be calling the name of a friend in the eternal ear of our heavenly Father. Intercession indicates involvement.

Thanksgiving. "In everything give thanks, for this is the will of God in Christ Jesus concerning you" (I Thess. 5:18). Feeling thankful is an act of the emotions. Giving thanks is an act of the will. In many circumstances we may not "feel" thankful. However, with a will bent to the will of the Father we can in all things "give thanks." The way to be glad is to be grateful. In this matter the will has to superimpose itself on the feelings. Fortunately feelings change. They can be converted to follow the will. It is in these emotional deserts that we can show our true devotion by offering the "sacrifice of thanksgiving" (Psalms 116:17). This is thanksgiving that comes willingly, though not easily.

Our phone rang during dinner. My wife answered as our children and I listened to her end of the conversation. It was our pediatrician calling to express thanks for a gift. Over and over my wife said words like, "You have given us so much... you have done so much for us...we love you...we owe you so much...we are so thankful for you." When the conversation ended, one of our little girls, to whom God was very personal, asked with wide eyes, "Was that God?" She had been conditioned to perceive God as the Good Lord, the "giver of every good and perfect gift." It seemed only reasonable that such thanks should be offered Him. That is the way we should think of the Lord.

We have a tendency to omit thanksgiving from our prayers. We wait until something goes wrong and jump to petition. For example, when was the last time you thanked God for your liver? Not lately! Let something go wrong with it and see how soon it becomes a topic of prayer. Look around and lift up the many little things you take for granted. An attitude of gratitude will incline the heart to thanksgiving.

Have you thanked God lately for pain? It is a marvelous gift of God to help prevent us from further injuring ourselves. Dr. Paul Brand worked with persons having leprosy in Vellore, India. He related how persons with this disease have no feeling in the infected parts of their bodies. One of his patients at the Christian Medical College was given a weekend pass. In his tiny apartment he slept on a mat on the floor. He awakened the next morning to find his fingers bleeding. During the night rats had eaten part of his fingers without him feeling any pain. He resolved to stay awake the next night and kill the rat. He sat on the floor with a large club. By the light of a kerosene lamp he read until around 4:00 a.m. before falling asleep. When he awakened he noticed his hand had been resting on the lantern for over two hours without feeling any pain. Massive skin grafts were required.

Pain is most often a super signal to let us know something is wrong and needs to be cared for. Thank God for your pain mechanism. An analysis of your prayers of thanksgiving is an autopsy of your soul. It reveals your spiritual condition. It betrays your attitude toward God. A prayer life lacking in thanksgiving reveals a spiritual life lacking in a proper understanding of the Lord. "For He is good; for His mercy endureth forever." Common courtesy prompts expressions of thanks.

Years ago William Law posed a question and answered it

himself: "Who is the greatest saint? It is not the one who prays most or who does most, it is the one who is most thankful."

Praise. Through the Psalmist the Lord revealed, "Whosoever offereth praise glorifieth Me" (Psalms 50:23). Praise is a convergence of worship and thanksgiving. In worship we acknowledge Who God is. In thanksgiving we acknowledge what He has done. These twin flames melt our hearts into praise.

A spirit of praise enables you to change your prayer from "Lord, when am I going to get out of this?" to "Lord, what am I to get out of this?" Trials and tribulations when viewed through a praise-oriented outlook become gold mines from which we get some of life's greatest treasures.

Praise will not allow a person to make a prolonged emotional pit stop. Many persons exclaim how they love to read the book of Psalms because it is uplifting. An analysis of many of the Psalms will reveal the writer starts by expressing a state of despondency or depression. He then moves to praising the Lord. As a natural-supernatural consequence, his spirit soon is seen to soar on wings of elation. Thus, externals conducive for depression are overcome by the internal spirit of praise. This is in keeping with an underlying theme of the New Testament. Throughout is the thesis, "I will put within you all that is necessary for a joyous and productive life. This joy is not contingent upon externals." Realizing this gives birth to a spirit of praise. Praise breaks the golden handcuffs of materialism. It frees a person of materialism. As the spirit soars above things to the throne of God, tangible things are put in perspective. Preoccupation with the Source supplants inordinate occupation with substance.

Two stimuli to praise are scripture and song. Read the praise passages as a prayer. Obtain a good hymn book and use it in the same way even if you can't sing. Let the words from these two sources guide the thought and intent of your heart.

Persons prone to praise Him are not inclined simply to come before Him when they have a new celestial shopping list.

In Queensland, Australia there lived some impoverished workmen who sought to eke out a living on a poor plot of land. They lived in poverty not knowing that beneath their feet buried under their infertile soil was the largest gold deposit in the world. They lived as paupers in bread lines with gold deposits of inestimable value right under them.

Pity not these penniless, destitute farmers for not using their assets. An even greater waste is the wealth of spiritual blessings available through prayer--unmined treasuries. Don't let a neglect of prayer be your untapped resource of spiritual wealth.

3
"IN THIS MANNER, THEREFORE, PRAY"

Jesus Christ kept the communication channel open between Himself and the throne-room of heaven. The gospels record fifteen occasions when He prayed.

In launching His public ministry He prayed when baptized. His prayer opened heaven in a distinct way never before or since experienced. As John baptized Him and He prayed, the Holy Spirit descended on Him in the form of a dove as the voice of the Father was heard to say, "This is my beloved Son in whom I am well pleased."

John the Baptist in that moment held God the Son in his hand, heard God the Father with his ears, and saw God the Holy Spirit with his eyes.

All of Christ's great works were accompanied by prayer. His miracles were wrapped in prayer. His last breath was a prayer: "Father, into Thy hands I commend My spirit" (Luke 23: 46).

By His example He inspired His disciples to want to know how to pray. As our role model, we should follow His example in prayer. By His practice and by His proclamation, He has commended prayer.

In response to a request from His disciples He left us a model prayer. Evidently He taught this prayer on several occasions. Matthew records it in a form worthy of our consideration (Matt. 6: 9 - 13). Christ said we are to pray "In this manner..." That is, we don't have to pray these exact words, though that in itself is admirable. However, in praying we should include the various parts of this prayer.

As Jehovah decreed the design for the tabernacle to Moses, so Christ prescribed the pattern of prayer for us. The law was written by the hand of God the Father. This lesson on prayer came from the lips of God the Son.

GOD'S NATURE

Four characteristics of God's nature are self-evident in the model.

HIS ROLE - "Our Father"

The title "Father" speaks of birth. In the spiritual world there are only two potential fathers. Jesus in rebuttal to a group of blood-thirsty religious leaders said, "If God were your Father, you would love Me, for I proceeded forth and came from God; nor have I come of Myself, but He sent Me...You are of your father the devil, and the desires of your father you want to do" (John 8:44).

For this reason the Bible speaks of a second birth. Paul gave a simple explanation to a small band of Christians of how one becomes a child of God: "For you are all sons of God through faith in Christ Jesus" (Galatians 3:26). It is "through faith in Christ."

In understanding a word it is helpful to know how it was used at the time of its employment. Hebrews 11:1 defines faith for us: "Now faith is the substance of things hoped for, the evidence of things not seen." The Greek word translated "substance" is HYPOSTASIS. From the pages of antiquity comes the story of a lady who lost a court decision in contesting the ownership of a piece of land. She appealed her case to a higher court. Archaeologists found the documents of her appeal recently. In her letter to the court she said, "In order that my lord the judge may know that my appeal is just, I attach my title deed (HYPOSTASIS)." "Faith" is the title deed to our kinship with the Father.

Two things are essential to new birth: "...repentance toward God, and faith toward our Lord Jesus Christ" (Acts 20: 21).

Repentance involves:

* Conviction. There must be an awareness of sin and need of a Savior.

* Contrition. Godly sorrow for sin and a desire to have something done about it is a must.

* Correction. There must be a correcting of one's life course. This involves a turning from sin and a turning to Christ.

Faith involves:

* Acceptance of facts. Not all facts needed are known initially, but a simple knowledge that salvation comes through the person of Jesus Christ is a starting point. As faith becomes more informed, it believes in the virgin birth, the virtuous life, the vicarious death, the victorious resurrection, and the valedictory ascension. A person may believe all this and still not be saved.

A person desiring to invest in a bank may inquire of its security. Having a basic knowledge of accounting, the potential investor is even shown the auditor's notes and concludes the bank is sound. A review of the safety procedures may lead to the conclusion the bank is physically secure. The possible investor knowing all these facts may attest to these truths and walk out with his or her money in hand. That isn't faith. At this point the person has only accepted the facts.

Faith involves trusting the person also. Only when the likely depositor fills out a deposit slip and hands it and the money to the teller for deposit has the bank been trusted.

In faith resulting in salvation more than mere facts about Christ and the Bible are necessary. One might ascribe to many commendable facts about Him and not be saved. Only when He is trusted as a person is salvation a reality.

Once the deposit is made that which is deposited is the responsibility of the bank. In this light, one who invests faith in Christ as Savior can declare: "I know whom I have believed, and am persuaded that he is able to keep that which I have committed unto him against that day" (II Timothy 1:12).

Faith is the single way to the Father.

Suppose two persons, one a Christian and the other not, were locked in a cell block with steel reinforced concrete walls one mile thick. Imagine their entrance way sealed solid its entire length. There isn't a thing necessary for salvation that the believer can't tell that person in that tiny inner chamber. There isn't a thing necessary to salvation that lost person can't do in order to be born again. Faith that produces obedience is the only requirement for becoming a child of God and being able to pray "Our Father..."

Jesus has introduced us to God with this single significant statement "Our Father..." This is the most hope-inspiring phrase known to mankind. With only one exception every prayer of Christ's was introduced with the title "Father." That one exception was on the cross when He prayed "My God, My God..." There with the sin of the world on Him He was separated from the Father.

In giving this model Jesus would have used the Aramaic "ABINU" for "our Father." It comes from the same root as ABBA, a title of loving dependance. "Our" is an acknowledgement of the brotherhood of all believers.

HIS RIGHTEOUSNESS - "Hallowed be Thy name"

This prayer begins with concern for God's welfare even before our own needs. "Hallowed be thy name" comes first and establishes our priority as being God's need above our own.

"Hallowed" comes from the Greek verb HAGIAZO. The noun form is HAGIOS and means "holy." This means His name is sacred.

There is a blasphemy among the saints which is more dangerous than that of the streets. It is in humanizing God and approaching Him as a casual equal. If His name is hallowed in the heart, it will be holy on the lips and in the life.

In the Bible era a name was more than a mere title by which one was identified. It was an expression of a person's nature. For that reason when a person underwent a dramatic change in life his or her name was often changed.

To hallow the name of God means to honor, respect, and glorify Him. We do this when we have a humble heart, a sweet spirit, an attitude of gratitude, and glorify Him by our lifestyle.

In ancient Israel the name of Jehovah was considered so hallowed that Jews would not pronounce or spell it. Instead they used a four-lettered tetragram, JHWH.

A knowledge of the meaning of some of the Old Testament names applied to the Father help us to see how hallowed His name really is. He was called "El" meaning "the Mighty One." Often other titles are derived by combining this prefix with other expressions, such as, "Elohim" which refers to His power; "Elyon" meaning "the Most High," and "El-Shaddai," "God Almighty." "Adonai" identifies Him as "my Master." "Jehovah" speaks of His eternal nature. From the meaning of these titles we see why His name should be hallowed. The glory of God's great name must take supersedence over all things.

Martin Luther posed a question and answered it. "How is

God's name hallowed among us? When our doctrine and nature are truly Christian."

When we hallow His name we are praising His very nature as revealed to us. Romans 1 says nature reveals His nature. Georgia's poet laureate, Sidney Lanier expressed such praise in his work, "The Marshes of Glynn." Any person who has ever driven across theses marshes on the way to Jekyll Island can relive their beauty:

"As the marsh-hen secretly builds on the watery sod,
Behold I will build me a nest on the greatness of God:
I will fly in the greatness of God as the marsh-hen flies.
In the freedom that fills all the space twixt the marsh and the skies."

HIS RULE - "Thy kingdom come"

The prayer concludes with the expression, "Thine is the kingdom and the power and the glory forever."

When we pray "Thy kingdom come", we are simply affirming we want His rule in our lives. The kingdom of God is any territory over which He rules. If He rules over your life that is His domain; He is the Monarch, the King.

To pray "Thy kingdom come" means the same as "I pledge allegiance." It is a way of saying, "I want to be your loyal subject."

Napoleon Bonapart said, "There are only two forces in the world --spiritual force and material force, and spiritual force always wins." Tragically, in his role as a leader he never aligned himself with the spiritual force. He never submitted the empire over which he ruled to the Kingdom of God.

"Kingdom" translates BASILEIA which literally means "rule" or "reign." It is a way of saying "God, I want you to be in charge of my life."

The Jewish Talmud, which is a commentary on Scripture,

says that a prayer in which there is no mention of the kingdom of God is not a prayer (Berakoth 21a).

Jesus taught us that we are to seek "first the kingdom of God, and His righteousness" (Matt. 6: 33). When seeking for and praying for the kingdom you need to know what it is you are desiring. Paul said, "The kingdom of God is not food and drink, but righteousness, and peace, and joy in the Holy Spirit."

So deceptive is the world's father, the Devil, that he has folks looking everywhere for peace and joy except where it is found. In the process he has twisted human thought to the point where it is believed that the one source, that is, God's kingdom is an unpleasant one.

There are three ways in which His kingdom comes:

The conversion of the lost.

The compliance with His Word by the saved.

The coming of the King to His kingdom.

HIS RIGHT - "Thy will be done"

This expresses a desire for God's will to be done as completely on earth as it is continually in heaven.

Watchman Nee is quoted as having said, "He does not ask us to support His cause, but to submit to His will." That is summed up in this portion of the model prayer.

We can't pray for His will to be done if we are disobedient to His word. To pray for it to be done necessitates a commitment to doing. Not to be so committed is to pray as impractical as a person who hides in a storm shelter made of styrofoam painted to look like stone.

Be not as Plutarch said of the Greeks, "They knew what was just, but did it not."

Selfish persons can't pray this portion of the prayer. To pray it means to make God's cause a priority over your own concerns. It means to pray, "God, I truly want what you want more than what I want."

When we reach the mind-set of David, we gain joy. He grew to say, "I delight to do Thy will, O my God" (Ps. 40:8).

The Roman Seneca, though perhaps lacking in some Bible understanding, nevertheless, commented: "I have trained myself not only to obey God, but to agree with His decisions. I follow Him because my soul wills it. Not because I must." When the will of the Father becomes our ambitious desire we have a fresh new view of life.

To pray this portion of the prayer is to say, "God, I want your best for me. I want your plan for my life fulfilled."

I saw a cartoon recently depicting a couple looking over a calendar as the wife is saying, "Remember God loves you and everybody else has a wonderful plan for your life." In a day of a proliferation of plans for your life there is one that is right and rewarding. It is the will of the Father.

The same Jesus who taught us that "Whosoever shall do the will of God, the same is my brother, and my sister, and my mother..." (Mark 3:35), AND then He went out and modeled the prayer in the garden on the evening of His execution as He prayed "Thy will be done."

We too need to pray that Gethsamene proviso: "Thy will..."

Jesus knew what the will of the Father was when He prayed this prayer. It wasn't a request for insight, but for strength to do the Father's will. He was committed to the Father's will.

We too need to pray that Gethsamene proviso: "Thy will..."

He has the right for His will to be done. He doesn't force it; He wants to win because He is right not because of His might.

Investigate people like Florence Nightingale, Joan of Arc, Francis of Assisi, Lincoln, Wilberforce, Queen Victoria, Schweitzer, Laubach, Lottie Moon, and Billy Graham and you will find they prayed, "Thy will be done."

OUR NEED:
The prayer not only deals with God's nature but our need. Basically our needs can be summed up in three expressions.

FOR PROVISIONS -"Give us this day...bread"
The words "us" and "our" exclude selfishness. We are to be mindful of others in all things.

The late Robert McCracken, of Riverside Church in New York, said: "The prayer of intercession is the noblest form of Christian prayer, for in it love and imagination reach their highest and widest range."

"Bread" is a summary word for food in general but also for all provisions. Some folks find it hard to realize the need to pray this portion of the prayer when the freezer is stocked, the pantry full, and there are no family members in the hospital. We who have our daily bread acknowledge Him as the source when we pray this segment. "Every good and perfect gift is from above..." (James 1:17). The request is for "daily bread." This helps us to wait confidently on the Lord and avoid selfishness.

One old saint was asked by a skeptic, "Why don't you pray for tomorrow's bread also?" Her response is classic, "Because God doesn't deliver stale bread." He has a daily delivery.

This prayer is to be offered before and after honest labor. It doesn't encourage indolence or a slovenly work ethic. It is an acknowledgment that God is the one who gives us the ability to get what we need.

FOR PARDON - "Forgive us our debts as we forgive..."
Jesus followed this by saying, "For if you forgive men their

trespasses, your heavenly Father will also forgive you. But if you do not forgive men their trespasses, neither will your Father forgive your trespasses" (Matthew 6: 14, 15).

In summary, this means the unforgiving are unforgiven because they are unforgivable.

Reputedly, Leonardo da Vinci painted the head of his worst enemy on the shoulders of Judas when painting the "Last Supper." That night afforded him a restless sleep. The next day as he tried to paint the face of Christ he couldn't gain a clear concept of what He should look like. Finally he went back and painted out the face of his enemy as representative of Judas. Instantly he gained a concept of what Christ should look like. The act represented his forgiveness of his nemesis.

Employ Ephesians 4: 30 - 32: "And grieve not the Holy Spirit of God, whereby ye are sealed unto the day of redemption. Let all bitterness, and wrath, and anger, and clamor, and evil speaking, be put away from you, with all malice: And be ye kind one to another, forgiving one another, even as God for Christ's sake hath forgiven you."

An unforgiving spirit is a major obstacle to a productive prayer life. When it is difficult to forgive someone remember what all Christ has forgiven you of and out of gratitude forgive your peer.

John Calvin evidently realized this. He and Martin Luther often contested one another. Regarding one heated circumstance Calvin said, "Though he call me a devil a thousand times, yet will I love and honor him as a precious servant of Christ." Calvin had a 70 times 7 complex; unlimited forgiveness.

OUR PROTECTION - "Lead us not into temptation..."

This statement must be interpreted in light of James 1: 13, "Let no man say when he is tempted, I am tempted of God;

for God cannot be tempted with evil, neither tempteth he any man."

Further James explained, "Every man is tempted, when he is drawn away of his own lust, and enticed" (James 1: 14).

Jesus gave us a defense technique when He instructed us to "Watch and pray, that ye enter not into temptation" (Matt. 26: 41).

This is an acknowledgment that temptation and evil result in what is not good for us or glorifying for God. Therefore, there is an abhorrence of it and a desire to be spared of it. This is a plea to be kept out of the danger zone. It shows a growing repulsion of sin. Deliver us from the evil one.

Evil desires to engulf the purest, cling to the holiest, shadow the brightest, and embitter the happiest. All evil gets its pedigree from hell. It calls Satan father. Therefore, to spare us its misery Jesus lovingly taught us to, "Watch and pray, that ye enter not into temptation" (Matt. 26:41).

The conclusion of the prayer gives us courage - "Thine is the ...power." He has the power to deliver us. Remember these words: "There hath no temptation taken you but such as is common to man: but God is faithful, who will not suffer you to be tempted above that ye are able; but will with the temptation make a way to escape, that ye may be able to bear it" (I Cor. 10:13).

That way is open to all who can legitimately pray "Our Father..."

4
HOW YOU CAN HELP RUN
THE UNIVERSE

"There is no greater peace than that which comes from prayer and no greater fellowship than to join in prayer with others," said former President George Bush in addressing the National Association of Religious Broadcasters.

Abraham Lincoln confided to a close friend: "I have been driven many times upon my knees by the overwhelming conviction that I had nowhere else to go." During one of the many dark hours of his presidency a friend saw Mr. Lincoln sitting before a great fireplace with his elbows on his knees and his face in his hand. The friend listened attentively as the president prayed without knowing there was anyone listening, "Oh God, oh God, help me, I cannot lead these people without your help, without you."

These men revealed they needed divine guidance in leading this nation. Their roles as world rulers are important. However, each of us has a sphere of influence - a territory over which we exert leverage. We must be as faithful as they in our quarter. God's help is needed in our lives in order for Him to rule the universe through us.

It is impressive to note that presidents have a need to pray and find comfort in it. Even more impressive is it to observe our Lord Jesus Christ engaged in prayer and commended us to do it.

Jesus taught His disciples to pray. They did not ask Him how to conduct a committee meeting. They did not ask for insight into business meetings. They inquired, "Lord, teach us to pray." His example had been such they wanted to follow it.

S.D. Gordon wrote, "The greatest thing you can do for God and man is to pray. You can do more than pray after you have prayed, but you cannot do more than pray until you have prayed."

Our impetuous nature prompts us to want to be doers above all else. We put in longer hours, work smarter not harder, employ the latest labor-saving equipment, and expand the work force in efforts to do more. Gordon suggests that the productivity multiplying element is prayer. Our tendency is to pause and pray when all else fails. Fewer things would fail if they were initiated through prayer. God is not going to let His will fail.

Andrew Murray remarked, "We must begin to believe that God, in the mystery of prayer, has entrusted us with a force that can move the heavenly world, and can bring its power down to earth."

That means you can cooperate with God in running the universe. Find His will and pray "Thy will be done..." Remember, it is "Thy will be done," not "My will be done," or "Thy will be changed."

Prayer is either the greatest thing we ever do or it is among the cruelest of hoaxes.

PRAYER IS NOT:
A supernatural credit card.
A magic wand to wave to keep evil away or a lucky rabbit's foot to bring good fortune.

An opiate to tranquilize nervous Christians.

A campaign to persuade God of something.

Arm wrestling with God.

Samuel Zwemer observed: "True prayer is God the Holy Spirit talking to God the Father in the name of God the Son, and the believer's heart is the throne room."

Thomas Goodwin, a Puritan, wrote, "The Holy Spirit who is the intercessor within us, and who searches the deep things of God, doth offer, prompt, and suggest to us in our prayers these very things that are in God's heart, to grant the thing we desire of Him, so as it often comes to pass that a poor creature is carried on to speak God's very heart to Himself, and then God cannot, nor doth deny..." the request we make of Him.

The Holy Spirit works in our lives like an electric monitor that is constantly scanning in search of a designated signal. Once the beam is located, the monitor locks on allowing the person to follow the signal to its source. When we lock on to the heart beat of God it then remains for us simply to pray the sublime prayer "Thy will be done..."

There are 953 scriptures which mention prayer. If Satan can obscure these or misdirect our understanding of any one of them, he has succeeded in a vital way. Guy H. King wrote, "No one is a firmer believer in the power of prayer than the devil; not that he practices it, but that he suffers from it."

By subtle design Satan still endeavors to pervert what God has provided. Prayer is one area he has contaminated with great effectiveness. There are two equal and opposite dangers. One is neglect of prayer. The other is excesses in prayer. Rarely is the extreme in the amount of time spent praying. Most often it relates to technique.

Time spent in prayer is time invested in eternity. Professing not to have enough time to pray is a revelation of improper priorities.

Robert Murry McCheyne, who made it a practice not to see the face of a man each day until he had seen the face of God, said, "I ought to spend the best hours of the day in communication with God. It is my noblest and most fruitful employment..."

Designate a set time to pray and preserve it as though it were an appointment with the president of the United States. It being more important than such a prestigious appointment should be protected even more zealously.

Our technique in prayer is equally important. Satan has distorted true prayer to the point of confusion. Many are disappointed because they think it is to be an exercise in ecstasy. When the wished for emotional high doesn't consistently happen, they become disillusioned and stop praying. Vain repetition, under the guise of fervor, is a deception. Ritualistic practice is a delusion. "Saying" a prayer is improper. Even if it is the model prayer, it should never be simply said, but prayed. That is, the fire beneath it must be rekindled if the same soup is to be savory. Some persons even become more concerned about their posture than their prayer. They go heavy on style, such as, praying with hands outstretched, uplifted, and/or folded. It is the heart not the hands about which our Lord is concerned.

A commendable technique to employ in prayer is to combine it with Bible reading. When you come to a passage that ignites your mind, turn it into a prayer. It being His Word, you know it is His will -- pray it. Prayer should be the fullest revelation of knowledge of Scripture.

PRAYER IS:
Conversation with God.
A warm, intimate relationship with God.
Jesus said we can address God as "Abba." This was an Aramaic word for intimacy. It was a word used of a little, totally

dependent, loving child of an adored father.

Archbishop Temple wrote: "The essential act of prayer is not the bending of God's will to ours, but the bending of our wills to His. The proper outline of a Christian's prayer is not 'Please do for me what I want,' but 'Please do in me, with me, and through me what you want.'"

DOES GOD ANSWER PRAYER?:

Emphatically He does. Some have said He either answers "Yes, No, or Wait A While."

God having made human beings must have a sense of humor. That being true, I think His response to some of our prayers must be "Hey, wait a minute, which one of us is God!"

Seriously, I think one of His answers is, "No, I am not going to give you that. I am going to give you something better."

Isaiah encourages us by reminding us that "...the Lord waits to be gracious to you..." (Isaiah 30:18). This should give you a wonderful sense of being loved.

I John 5: 13, 14 is the code which allows you to participate in running the universe. It involves:

I. COMPLIANCE "if we ask"

Many of our failures result from our not asking. When we think of a tragedy, we usually think of something that happened. There is another form of tragedy. It is when something good that might have happened doesn't happen. Many answers to prayers aren't granted because the prayer isn't offered. What we are may not be a tragedy. The tragedy may be that we are not what we might well be if submitted to His will.

It is of course conditional, but Jesus said, "Ask and it shall be given you." Conversely, if you don't ask, you don't get. To ask is to reveal a spirit of dependence, reliance, and trust. It shows confidence in the Lord.

God wants to do His will. He often waits to be asked in order to evidence He is not superimposing His will on unwilling subjects. In His sovereign will He has chosen not to violate our free will. Therefore, ask Him to perform His will through you.

II. CONFIDENCE   "this is the confidence we have in Him"

You can be assured your prayers are heard. Observe, "He hears us." The term used means He "favorably hears" us.

The word "confidence" actually means "boldness." When you know you are praying according to God's will, you can be bold in your prayer-life.

Civil War General William Tecumseh Sherman wrote DeWitt Talmadge upon the death of his beloved wife, "I am sure that you know that the God who created the minnow, and who molded the rose and the carnation giving each its sweet fragrance, will provide for those mortal men who strive to do right in this world which He has stocked with birds, animals, and men. At all events I will trust Him with absolute confidence." That is an expansion on the truth that if a sparrow can't fall to the earth without being noticed by our Heavenly Father, we can be confident of His watchful and attentive care.

Faith is confidence in God's character. To believe that God keeps His word is to be confident of His care. As the sun melts frost off a window and lets it become a clear medium through which to enlighten an inner chamber, so confidence enables us to understand God's working.

III. CONDITION   "according to His will"

The key is can you ask what you are requesting for Jesus' sake. That is, in order that He might be glorified by it. Will it please Him?

Some few devout persons spend time talking to God and then being attentive to His inaudible voice, that is, they meditate and willfully open their minds to Him. Such persons are trying to be attentive to God. This is commendable. The process should be reversed. We should make ourselves open and attentive in order to first know His will so that we can then request it.

Oliver Wendell Holmes noted the trouble with our minds is that they are like checking accounts, and the reason we are overdrawn is that we haven't put anything in it. Often we pray without letting God make a deposit. This takes time. We dare not swagger out ahead of God. Zephaniah reminds us of our Lord's basic rule, "Therefore, wait for me," says the Lord (Zeph. 3:8).

In the model prayer our Lord instructed us to pray "Thy will be done" (Matt. 6: 10). Candidly, I sometimes don't find His will clearly revealed. In those moments, as in all others, a worthy prayer is "Thy will be done." He knows what His will is even if we don't.

If we do not know His will before we pray, we should pray with the Gethsemane proviso, "Thy will be done."

In Acts 11 there is an experience in the life of Peter which demanded he demonstrate what he had done was the will of God. His life was in danger because he had violated four basic ritualistic taboos. Scripture notes the religious leaders "contended" with him. That means they threatened his life. This was not an academic debate; it was verbal war. Peter had eaten with a Gentile. The food was that of a Gentile. This Gentile was a Roman. Peter stayed in the home after dark. All four of these things were against tradition. As Peter "explained" to them the reason for his conduct, he reveals to us seven principles he used to determine God's will.

First, he engaged in prayer.(Vs. 5). This was not self-deluding rationalization. It was petitioning God for His will to be known and done. This was the point of beginning and ending, but it was not all that he did.

Second, Peter was thinking; he employed his mental capacity (Vs. 6). The expression "I considered" meant "to put your mind on something, to ponder." This referred to thinking through in great detail. That is the reason our Lord has given us a mind.

Third, the word of God was given rapt attention. Peter actually heard the voice of God (Vs. 7). In that era God occasionally spoke to Spirit-filled believers with an audible voice. Today He has elected to give us His word in a written form rather than audible. Peter heard the word three times before it sank in. Keep filling your mind with God's Word in order to have a more effectual prayer life.

Fourth, providential circumstances were considered. While Peter was praying and considering God's word, three men suddenly appeared with a special request (Vs. 11). This was something more than coincidental circumstances. If circumstances ever suggest something contrary to God's Word, they are not of God.

Fifth, the Holy Spirit gave Peter a compulsion which complied with God's Word (Vs. 12). The Holy Spirit will never lead anyone to do anything contrary to God's Word. The expression "the spirit bade me go" is equivalent to the teaching ministry of the Holy Spirit through the Holy Bible.

Current confusion consequences when persons say "the Holy Spirit told me." That leaves no room for a Spirit-filled friend to respond. Rebuttal is tantamount to arguing with God. Misuse of the phrase is a super-pious cop-out. It is drawing God in on your side without the benefit of other insight.

Sixth, comparisons were made by Peter and the three men (Vss. 13 - 15). Upon comparing notes their insights dove-tailed.

This convergence of thought was of God. This is a further reference to thinking. Remember, the human mind is there for a purpose and when guided by Scripture is reliable.

Seventh, scripture memorization, was applied (Vs. 16). Peter recalled the Word of God as recorded in Isaiah 44: 3 and applied it. Under pressure it is the Word of God which you know that gives stability.

Three further considerations for finding God's will are offered.

State your commitment to God's will even before it is known. Pre-commitment is essential. Two examples reveal why. Both Gideon and Saul prayed for God to reveal His will to them.

Gideon used a fleece (Judges 6: 36, 37) in his quest for God's will. He asked the Lord to be pleased to give him a physical indication of His will. The Lord revealed His will to him.

"When Saul inquired of the Lord, the Lord answered him not..." (I Samuel 28: 6).

Why did God answer one and not the other?

Saul sought God's will in a rebellious state of mind. He would not have done it if he had known it. Wisdom reveals "One who turns away his ear from hearing the law, even his prayer shall be an abomination" (Proverbs 28: 9). Saul was such a person and individuals of that temperament do not have an effective prayer life.

Gideon was eager to know and DO God's will. Hence, the Lord was pleased to reveal it to him.

Start with the known. Do what you know to do before asking for more to do. It is like playing an instrument. You must master one lesson before going on to the next. There are certain parts of God's will He has made very clear. Check yourself on these known factors:

A. Your salvation. God is "not willing that any should perish but that all should come to repentance" (II Peter 3:9).

B. Your sanctification. This means to be set aside for His use. "For this is the will of God, even your sanctification..." (I Thessalonians 4: 3).

C. Your sexuality. "For this is the will of God...that you should abstain from fornication" (I Thessalonians 4: 3).

D. Your sacrifice. God appeals to us to "...present your body a living sacrifice...that ye may prove what is that good, and acceptable, and perfect, will of God." (Romans 12:1,2)

E. Your stewardship. Jesus said you "...ought to tithe" (Matthew 23: 23). It is simply His will for all of His children to give one-tenth of their income through the local church.

F. Your subjection. "Submit yourselves to every ordinance of man for the Lord's sake...For this is the will of God..." (I Peter 2: 13 - 15).

G. Your spirit. Our spirit should be such that motivates us to maintain an attitude of gratitude. "In everything give thanks; for this is the will of God in Christ Jesus concerning you" (I Thessalonians 5: 18).

Sustain your search. God guides in increments.

A. He guides consecutively. He leads us step by step. Patience and persistence are twin virtues in following Him. "The steps of a good man are ordered of the Lord: and he delights in his way" (Psalms 37: 23).

B. He guides completely. He is faithful who has promised "I will instruct thee and teach thee in the way which thou shalt go; I will guide thee..." (Psalms 32: 8).

C. He guides cooperatively. "For as many as are led by the Spirit of God, they are the sons of God" (Romans 8: 14).

The Greek word translated "led" is AGO. It does not refer to an inanimate object, like a sled, which must be drug. It is used of a well-trained and obedient animal that responds to the slightest tug by its master's leash. If we will cooperate, He will lead.

Prayer is not the means for getting man's will done in heaven, but for getting heaven's will done on earth. Consent to His will even if you don't know it specifically in an instance.

IV. THE CONSEQUENCE   "we have the petitions"

It may be a future certainty, but it is a certainty. However, the verb tense used means in the moment we ask anything according to His will, we have it. It is loaded on God's divine delivery van at that moment. It may take it a while to be delivered, but delivery is assured.

Sometimes the time lapse between the request and delivery is such that we forget the delivery is the result of the request. This principle of deferred delivery often causes us not to connect it with a specific prayer. A prayer log with requests noted and dated can help jog your memory and increase your joy. Provide in the left hand column a space for the date of the request to be entered. Allow adequate space for the request to be noted. In the right margin allow for the date of delivery to be entered. Also leave space for you to note your reaction to the answer to the prayer.

5
A TIME TO PRAY AND A
TIME TO PLAY

The University of Georgia was playing the University of
Kentucky in Lexington. At stake for Georgia was a potential
National Football Championship. The contest was to be decid-
ed in the closing seconds. Kentucky was leading by two points.
UGA had driven within field goal range as the final seconds
ticked away. Georgia had no more time outs. Their All-Ameri-
can field goal kicker, Rex Robinson, was on the field when
Coach Dooley noticed he had only ten players on the field.
His dilemma was seemingly unresolvable. If he called time
out, the team would be penalized putting them out of field goal
range. If the kick was good, it would be disallowed because
of not having enough men on the field. Coach Dooley said, "I
looked around to see who wasn't in the game. Standing next to
me was my big tackle, Tim. I thought I had heard all excuses
when I asked, 'Tim, what in the world are you doing?' I wasn't
prepared for his response." "Coach," he said, "I'm praying."
Just then Coach Dooley looked back toward the field as the
official blew his whistle signaling time out. Turning to Tim he
exclaimed, "Man, you have some prayer life. Coach Curci just
called a time out to put pressure on Rex. Now get your big self

in the game and block." With Tim and his teammates blocking, the final seconds ticked away as the kick was up and good. Georgia won.

There is a time to pray and a time to play; a time to pray and a time to participate.

Jesus Christ taught us to pray. By precept and practical example He modeled prayer for us. If He needed to stay in touch with the Father through prayer, how much more do we need to do likewise?

How is your prayer-life?

I am persuaded that prayer is the main missing ingredient in modern Christianity. Many persons never pray until there is a major need. Few live in an attitude of prayer. God waits ambitiously to hear from us.

Christ appealed to us to "abide in me" (John 15:7). Paraphrased the entire passage is interpreted to mean: "If you stay in close touch with Me; and My words fill your mind, you won't want what I don't want. You will want what I want, and you will ask for it. When you do, I will give you what you and I want."

Some terms can better be described than defined. "Abide" is such a word. If you want to know what it means to abide, just watch two teens, a boy and a girl, who have just found one another. They know what it means to abide. They search for opportunities to talk to each other at school. They write each other notes. They send messages by friends. As soon as school is out and they get home, they pay homage to the teen's best friend, Alexander Graham Bell, by rushing to the phone to call and talk some more. It is a challenge to get them to hang up to eat, study, or go to bed. What they are saying is "Oh, dad, leave us alone we are abiding."

When married couples quit "abiding," their love-level is subsiding and often they start dividing. The same is true of prayer.

In a similar manner this occurs in our spiritual relationship with the Lord. Those who abide in Him in prayer are just as those teens in love striving to talk to each other. Abiding speaks of persistence.

* Prayer is the ladder down which God walks into our work and worship.

* Prayer is not a luxury -- not a duty -- not a storm shelter -- not a hospital -- it is simply fellowship with God; it is talking with the Lord.

* Prayer and Bible study are twin guides in finding God's will.

* Prayer is finding God's will and saying, "Thy will be done..." That is how you can work with God in running the universe.

* Prayer is like co-signing a check with God. He makes out the check on His heavenly account for the right amount, signs it, and waits for us to co-sign it by praying, "Thy will be done ..."

* Prayer is very much like an electric current. It needs a conductor or it is powerless. God's power often goes without release because there is no personal conductor called a person of prayer.

* Prayer seems to be the believer's last resort rather than the first resource.

We spend more time trying to pray sick Christians out of Heaven than we do praying lost sinners out of hell.

To get prayed for you have to check into the hospital. If you do, you automatically go on prayer lists.

The early church, lacking many of our resources, relied on prayer. Just think what would happen if we with our God-given resources would pray as they.

They had the fresh example of Christ and followed Him.

An example of a church at prayer is found in Acts 12:1-5. Herod the King was harassing the church. He killed James the brother of John. He then imprisoned Peter. Herod was merely waiting for a holy day to pass before executing Peter.

Peter was guarded by four squads of soldiers. That meant there were four groups of four guarding him on a rotating basis. He was bound and in a cell. Two guards stood outside and two were inside chained to him. What do you suppose was his anxiety level? Can you conceive of him being depressed under these conditions? Note his state of being as recorded in verse 6, "sleeping."

He wasn't worried. Worry is a pagan prayer. He probably lulled himself to sleep singing, "Don't worry -- be happy!"

Meanwhile --- back at the church there was a prayer meeting going on. An evaluation of this prayer meeting will give us insight into some proper characteristics of prayer. Note:

I. THE SPIRIT AVOWED Verse 5, It was "constant" prayer.

They didn't give up. A lack of response to their prayer didn't curtail their effort. They were persistent and willing to give God time to be God.

One Saturday afternoon my wife said, "I sure would like for US to grow some spinach for salads." I could hardly wait until half-time to go outside and start preparing the soil. It was late afternoon before I got the seed, but the sun set on a newly-planted spinach patch. During the next several weeks the sun and rain alternated in their effort to make that patch produce. I weeded and fertilized it affectionately. At best, however, it was about six weeks before we had any spinach.

During all that time my wife could have been saying, "He didn't even hear me. He doesn't care. He really doesn't love me."

Though I heard her, loved her, and went to work at once, it still took time to comply with her request and bring in a crop that would have made Popeye happy.

Often God goes to work in response to a specific prayer, but it still takes time. Give God time to be God.

For twelve years I prayed for our church to have a television ministry. During this time persons could have been saying, "God isn't hearing your prayer." For over five years I had been dealing directly with one station. Just as we finished a multi-million dollar building fund drive, I got a call from the station. They offered us the program time if we could start within a month. The cost? It was to be the most expensive hour on local television for any church in America. Having just committed themselves to fund a major building program, the church responded to an appeal to finance this new ministry. The Lord took twelve years to get us ready before He made the ministry a reality.

For fourteen years I prayed for our church to have a four thousand-seat worship center. The time-lag was necessary for the Lord to lead the people collectively to the necessary sacrificial will to be His agents of construction. Even after construction began three things developed any one of which could have stopped the project. Three "impossibilities" were shared with the congregation. It was appropriately stated that three identifiable miracles were needed. These were things that could not be achieved by natural means. Concerted prayer was offered regarding the three. Each in proper order became a supernatural reality. God's timing was perfect.

For twenty years I asked the Lord to be pleased to let me write a book. "A book?" He had something else in mind. It was like getting pickles out of a jar. Once the first one comes out the rest come easy. The Lord has been pleased to let me write fifteen books in the years following twenty years of prayer.

For twenty-one years I prayed that the Lord would grant us the joy of providing a home for unwed mothers. The court ruling regarding abortion virtually abolished such homes. If the Lord had answered the prayer initially, the home would have been short-lived. After twenty-one years of prayer, a friend who was unaware of this prayerful aspiration called. His mother-in-law who lived in a beautiful old southern home had died. He offered to sell the home to the church. These things always happen at impossible times. I explained we could not afford half the price he was asking. Prayer continued. A couple of days later he called and offered us more property, the house for half the original price, and he would finance the rest. We had our house. It was badly in need of repair, and we had no resources. We called on the Quartermaster of Eternity in prayer. He called on a ladies' group in the community that sponsors an annual decorators' show house. They phoned and asked if they could use the house as a decorators' show house. That involved builders and decorators refurbishing the house inside and out at no cost to us. Many of the decorators left their captivatingly beautiful furnishings for use by the home. The previous owner came in after the show house was over and developed a chapel in one room. A doctor and his wife funded air conditioning for the home. It took time for the Lord to convince our society of the sanctity of human life. Now our home flourishes.

For twenty-two years I prayed for our church to own and operate a radio station. I prayed for a specific station. When it was sold by the local owner to a New York syndicate and then to a Cleveland group, things looked bleak. Then when it unexpectedly came on the market, we didn't have money to purchase it. It was in a small prayer meeting I noticed a young lady show interest when I asked that we pray about it. Three days later I emerged from my office having had a conversation with the owner that seemed to indicate we had no chance of obtaining it. I asked my executive assistant for the phone number of the husband of the lady who had noted interest in such a ministry. "That's strange," said my assistant. "He just called and asked you to return his call." When I called him back, he explained how he had long had an interest in radio and graciously offered to help finance the venture. After twenty-two years the 10,000 watt station is now on the air debt-free.

It took time for God to be God.

One thing we often overlook or at least diminish in value is the benefit to be gained by the period between the request and the answer. That wait often draws us closer to God than the actual answer. During this incubation period, while God is very busy on our behalf, we have our attention focused on Him. Therefore, thank God for delays.

II. THE SOVEREIGN ADDRESSED - Verse 5, It was to "God".

Jesus taught us that when we pray we should pray, "Our Father..." (Matthew 6:9).

We often criticize persons who pray to or through intermediaries. Though that practice is not Scriptural we need to be cautious lest we make an opposite but equal mistake. When you pray, pray TO God, not just about something. Our attention is often given more to the thing about which we are praying than to the One to Whom we are praying.

Address Him as the Holy God He is with the respect He is due. Don't be casual in your style or flippant in your speech. Neither do you have to try to sound like you have a steeple in your throat or are speaking through a stained glass window.

When you pray remember which one of you is God. Prayer is a request, not an order.

III. THE SPECIFICS ANNOUNCED - Verse 5, It was

"for him".

Their prayer was very specific. When you pray, get down to the basic nitty and the fundamental gritty.

Specific prayers result in specific answers. A few years ago our church had reached an impasse in growth. We were land-locked. Unfortunately, through no fault of our neighbors several had become alienated. They had been approached improperly about selling their houses to the church and resented it. Resistance resulted. An impasse resulted in an impossible circumstance.

I arose early one morning while on a family retreat to Jekyll Island and walked the beach praying. Before the sun rose I knelt by a dune capped with a growth of sea oats to pray. Having predetermined it was God's will for the church to stay in this location and grow, I began to inventory our needs for the Lord just as though He didn't know them. I then implored Him just as though He needed it. One by one I explained to Him the houses needed and the order in which they were needed. I entreated Him to remove the barriers built up in hearts and provide the means for purchasing these houses. To have prayed for one house and for it to have become available might be considered a fluke. Two houses might have been evaluated as a coincidence. Three would have been looked upon as a streak of luck. Twenty-one! That's not a fluke, coincidence, or luck. It was a divine answer to specific prayer.

Don't think that by specific prayer you are going to embarrass God. When you know a thing to be His will, pray specifically about it. In answer to specific prayer God has an opportunity to reveal Himself.

The most earnest pray-er can't always know God's will in advance. Some say prayer that is not according to God's will is not true prayer. Not so. Many pray earnestly with a pure heart and holy intent but without a certainty regarding what they are praying about. You can pray for anything, whether you know it to be God's will or not. However, if it is not known to be His will it should be presented to Him with the willing contingency, "IF it is Your will, O Father." When prayer is subordinated to His will it shows trust of God. This is the Gethsamene prerequisite: "Thy will be done." By submitting your prayer in the envelope of "Thy will be done," you are happily leaving the choice to the God you trust. When this is done, the result should be interpreted in light of Romans 8:28: "And we know that all things work together for good to them that love God, to them who are the called according to his purpose."

IV. THE SOURCE APPOINTED - Verse 5, It was "the church".

The word "church" comes from the same root word as "Lord." The Greek word for Lord is KURIOS. The source for the word "church" is KURIACHE which means "those who belong to the kurios." It actually means "the people who belong to the Lord." Those belonging to the Lord are the ones given the right to address Him as "Our Father..."

Jesus said, "No man can come to the Father, but by Me" (John 14:6). This verse is most often understood regarding salvation. That is one vital application. It is also germane regarding prayer. Jesus gave us the right to approach the Father in His name. He authorized us to pray in His name; as His proxy. Regardless of the form or forum, Jesus only is our entree to the heart of the Father. Efforts to circumvent Him are futile. Attempts to pray apart from His name are like writing a counterfeit check. It doesn't work.

Many who do not belong to the Lord want to make requests of Him for temporal blessings, that is, things.

Not all prayers of those belonging to the Lord are heard. Often unconfessed sins will hinder the prayer-life. This will be developed in a subsequent chapter. If that is true, it is unreasonable for those who have never called on Him to forgive their sin to assume that He will answer their requests for things. They have neglected the proper use of the greatest thing He has offered them -- salvation.

The first prayer must be, "Lord, be merciful to me a sinner..."

A prayer of repentance involves:

* Agreeing with God about sin.
* Believing Jesus, the innocent One, died for us the guilty ones.
* Confessing your faith in Him as the One who can forgive your sin.
* Declaring your life to be yielded to Him as Savior.

The prayers of the church for Peter were answered directly and immediately. Peter was released from prison. His return to them marked the time to stop praying and start playing. So engaged were they in prayer that they found it difficult to disengage, accept the answer to their prayers, and go to work.

It just may be one type answer to prayer is "Yes, IF ..." In such a response the Lord is simply saying, "Yes, I will do my part as soon as you commit to or do your part." God is not going to expend wasted effort. There was a purpose in Him answering the prayers of the church and releasing Peter from prison. Knowing Peter's willingness to do His will, He released him to do his part.

The people in the prayer meeting were "astonished" at Peter's release. "Who would have thought it," was their reaction. Surprise, God kept His word and answered prayer. Instead the reaction should have been, "Now, isn't that just like the Lord. He kept His word."

"Many were gathered together praying" and among their number qualities qualifying for answered prayer converged.

Those "astonished" at the answer were beneficiaries of the faithfulness of the minority. This same factor works in churches today. There are many unfaithful Christians who benefit from the loving loyalty shown the Lord by their colleagues. The Lord blesses the faithful so much that their cup and saucer both overflow, and the less faithful receive the spill-over blessings. There are blessings inherent in group prayer.

Blessed answers to prayer are not to be ends in themselves, but means to an end. When the answer comes, it is time to quit praying and start playing. Get in the game.

6
PRAYER THERAPY

Prayer is neither a panacea nor a placebo. It is not a cure-all or a myth intended only to please. If it were a panacea, it would enable us to walk by sight and not faith. If it were a placebo, of all hoaxes it would be the most cruel. Of the many things prayer is, it is a formidable therapy. Innate in prayer is the power to cure many and varied ailments, both physical and emotional.

One of the primary purposes of prayer is to get as close to God as possible. It is a gift from Jesus to us whereby we can fine-tune our lives with the heartbeat of the Father. Though we tend to make prayer subjective, it is most fulfilling when it is objective and the object is our loving God. Preoccupation with Him in prayer enriches the pray-er and enables spiritual, emotional, and physical victory.

PROSEUCHE is the Greek word translated "prayer." It involves more than simply "saying a prayer." It is a general term which speaks of devotion and worship. Talking to the Lord in terms of reverence and adoration is a vital part of this worship. When most persons think of "prayer," they have in mind "supplication." That is, simply presenting a want-list to God. For many it is a time to express either sanctified complaints or specialized needs. Doing so is expedient. However, the real therapeutic advantages are to be gained through true PROSEUCHE, "prayer," that is, adoration, devotion, and worship of God.

Our "most fundamental need, duty, honor, and happiness," said the late Friedreich von Hugel, "is not petition, nor even contrition, nor again even thanksgiving...but adoration."

The word "adore" has become restricted almost exclusively to modern love songs. It implies the lover has been captivated by an overwhelming passion for the object of his or her obsession. True adoration of God is all that but more. It is reverent admiration, honor, and worship of Him as deity.

Not only has the word meaning been lost, but the awe and wonder of being in the presence of the Supernatural has been bleached out of life. The latest in special effects have been employed by the media to present pretentious encounters with extra-terrestrials as commonplace. A generation has grown up being exposed to this imaginary involvement with the supernatural. This has tended to devalue true Deity. This loss of the power of wonder from which adoration arises has left us less sensitive to the joy inherent in encountering God in prayer. We are all the more spiritually impoverished because of it. Intellectually and emotionally it has robbed us of a sense of wonder and respect. This looking upon the extraordinary as ordinary has left us without a sensitivity to the Supernatural. The degree to which this is true is the extent to which we have lost our ability to be strengthened within and renewed.

PRAYER AND RESTORATION

Our culture has become adapt at restoring old houses, cars, paintings, and other antiques. God is the supreme Restorer. David, one who was often physically exhausted, emotionally depleted, and spiritually defeated said, "He restoreth my soul..." (Psalm 23:3). Prayer is one of His most effective means of restoration.

Later when David's spiritual vitality was depleted by sin, he prayed, "Restore unto me the joy of thy salvation; and uphold me with thy free spirit" (Psalm 51:12).

Through the prophet Isaiah God declared, "I dwell in the high and holy place, with him also that is of a contrite and humble spirit, and to revive the heart of the contrite ones...I have seen his ways, and will heal him: I will lead him also, and restore comforts unto him and to his mourners" (Isaiah 57:15, 18). Jeanne is an example of this. Trembling with emotion she waited in her pastor's office for the attendants from the state mental health hospital to take her away. In those tense moments she began to talk more freely than ever about the real issue that had resulted in her condition. Descriptively she told of her sexual promiscuity. Tearfully she related how it was contrary to everything she had been taught and always believed. In the bearing of her soul it became apparent her emotional state was caused by guilt.

With compassion her pastor whom she trusted began to relate simple truths regarding forgiveness and the cleansing that consequents. Soon she was absorbed in what he was saying. Her glazed eyes began to focus as an evidence of her attentiveness. He then read: "If we confess our sins, he is faithful and just to forgive us our sins, and to cleanse us from all unrighteousness" (I John 1:9).

Jeanne was then asked, "Would you like to ask for and receive that cleansing?" "Oh, yes," she exuberantly exclaimed. Together they knelt and Jeanne opened her heart to the cleansing offer of Jesus Christ. With that the emotional shackles holding her captive proved to be made of ice and they melted away.

She arose with a smile followed by a joyous, emotional and tearful outburst. As she dried her tears, she sighed deeply and stood erect. The trembling was gone and she was perfectly composed. Just then the pastor's secretary buzzed. "The personnel from the mental hospital are here for Jeanne," she said. The pastor explained, "Jeanne, it's time to go. They are here for you."

"I don't need to go," she said confidently. In the time that followed, she, her mother, her pastor, and the personnel from the hospital all agreed she had no need of their help. The therapy of prayer had worked. The years following this experience verified her return to emotional health the instant her guilt was dealt with through prayer.

She had done as Jeremiah encouraged: "...Acknowledge your guilt..." (3:13). Though all restoration might not be as immediate and evident as Jeanne's, it is inevitable.

THREE DIMENSIONAL HEALING

A part of the Thessalonian benediction describes human beings as triads. "And the very God of peace sanctify you wholly; and I pray God your whole spirit and soul and body be preserved blameless unto the coming of our Lord Jesus Christ" (I Thess. 5:23). We are described as consisting of spirit, soul, and body. Rehabilitation is often needed in one or all of these areas.

When it was announced to the virgin Mary she would miraculously conceive and bear as a child the Son of God, she exclaimed, "My soul doth magnify the Lord, And my spirit hath rejoiced in God my Saviour" (Luke 1:46,47). She acknowledged her multi-faceted nature.

To understand this nature consider yourself as a two-story building. The lower floor is your physical body. The upper story has two windows. One, the soul, looks out upon things below, earthly things. The other, the spirit, is a skylight enabling you to look heavenward upon eternal spiritual truths. Bodily Mary acknowledged that from the bottom floor it was obvious much rejoicing was going on by virtue of what was happening in the light of the two windows.

Much has been written about healing of the body. This is perhaps to the neglect of the soul and spirit. Prayer can be used curatively in all three areas. The latter two need to be addressed.

PSYCHE is the New Testament word for "soul," the lower element of one's nature. For our purposes it is the basic life-force concerned primarily with the emotions. It denotes our immaterial part with its inferior powers which are held in common with animals, though on a more advanced and sophisticated plane. These traits include imagination, memory, understanding, and appetite.

PNEUMA in the Greek word for "spirit." It refers to the higher elements of our nature. It is the divine power added to the lives of human beings only. It speaks of our free will, power of reason, consciousness. These are some immortal traits evidencing we are created in the image of God. The spirit nature is part of a homo sapien's essence. No other creature possesses this eternal quality.

We have great difficulty differentiating between soul and spirit, but the Word of God has the capacity of "dividing asunder of soul and spirit" (Hebrews 4:12). To simplify our understanding of healing of part of our being other than the body, think of soul and spirit forming a synthesis of our temporal and eternal natures. Spiritual, bodily, and emotional healing are all aided by prayer therapy.

The matter of prayer and healing of the sick is dealt with in more detail elsewhere in this book. Summarily here it should be noted that James 5:15 declares, "The prayer of faith shall save the sick." The word for "sick" that is used refers to those who are weary and feeble from constant over-work. The word for "save" means they shall be given a state of rest. This includes more than just disease. It encompasses what is really needed more often, the renewal of a weary body.

Tensions of the body can be released through prayer therapy. There is physical release to be gained by being still and meditating on God and the things of God. What Paul prayed for his friends becomes our experience when we do. He prayed, "for this reason, I bow my knees before the Father, from whom every family in heaven and on earth derives its name, that He would grant you, according to the riches of His glory, to be strengthened with power through His Spirit in your inner man..." (Ephesians 3:14-16). This renews our physical being.

Hospitalized heart patients had fewer medical complications when prayed for, according to a carefully controlled, blind study reported in the Journal of the American Medical Association. The study was conducted by Dr. Randolph Byrd at the San Francisco General Medical Center's coronary care unit. He randomly assigned half of his 393 patients to either an "experimental" group or a "control" group. The health of group one was prayed for by three to seven born-again Christians and the other wasn't. Persons who were praying were told only the patient's first name and diagnoses, "along with pertinent updates in their condition." Dr. Byrd was kept uninformed of the progress until the data was completed. Records show the two groups were equally sick upon being admitted to the hospital. Statistics showed that the patients who were prayed for had fewer complications during their stay. In this, one of the most scientific of studies on prayer and healing, prayer was shown to be a vital factor. Even as a therapy unknown by the persons being prayed for, it was a significant help to recovery.

Even if prayer does not relieve pain, it helps to interpret it and make it more meaningful. Sir Thomas Lewis of the Christian Medical College in Vellore, India, often conducted experiments on consenting students. One purpose was to measure pain. A Sphygmomanometer Cuff, such as is used for taking blood pressure, was put on the student's arm. Compressed air was released in the cuff, cutting off the blood circulation instantly. A student would then be injected with a hypertonic saline solution in the forearm below the cuff and instructed to exercise his hand aggressively. With the oxygen cut off, lactic acid built up in the arm rapidly causing intense pain. Students were asked to rate the pain on a scale of one to ten. Most of them would classify it on the very high end of the scale.

In subsequent tests students were told there was a valve they could use to reduce the pressure instantly. Fresh blood carrying oxygen rushed into the arm causing a euphoric feeling. Upon learning they could control the pain, they became increasingly tolerant of it. Subsequent ratings of the same pain were much lower. The reason for the lower ratings was the knowledge that they were in charge of the pain. Through prayer great tolerance for pain can be gained by realizing that the One who loves you even more than you love yourself has His hand on your pain valve. Though the pain might not be relieved through prayer, its purpose can best be understood. An exceptional tolerance for pain can be developed through prayer.

Emotional health is also tied to prayer therapy. Anxiety, fear, and loneliness are three emotions which often need healing. They are often side effects of physical pain and suffering causing another form of suffering. Scripture and current conditions converge to show how prayer helps address needs in these areas.

ANXIETY

There is a slight but significant difference in anxiety and worry. According to its derivation, anxiety is a choking disquieting which is akin to anguish. Worry is more petty, restless, and expressed. Anxiety is often suppressed and silent. Worry is usually expressed to everyone. Both grow from the same seed. Worry grows up like the stalk of a weed. Anxiety grows down like a root, choking off all fertile thought.

Jesus appealed to His followers by saying, "Take no thought of tomorrow..." (Matthew 6:34). Let me rush to say He is not advocating a shiftless, thriftless, and thoughtless attitude. This is not an appeal to take a reckless crazy leap in the dark. Neither is He discouraging prudent planning. The expression is simply a prohibition against worry. As always, Jesus condemns foreboding while commending foresight.

MERIMNAO is the Greek word translated "thought." It is comprised of the word MERIZO meaning "to divide" with the suffix NOUS, meaning "mind." Therefore, it is the word for a divided mind. If Christ were saying the same truth today, it would be phrased "Don't worry!"

When we worry, the mind functions like a bio-computer. In controlling physical movement the mind imagines the move and bio-current flows to nerve ends activating the intended response. In controlling emotions, it functions similarly. A worry thought sends out bio-electrical energy through the nervous system to various glands. Glands so influenced cause secretions causing adverse physical and emotional reactions. Stress, fatigue, and physical illnesses can result. Knowing this adverse influence on the body resulted in Christ appealing to His followers not to worry. As at all times and in all things, He has His followers' interest in mind.

This same theme is amplified by Paul. Occasionally the archaic language of the Authorized King James causes us to have difficulty comprehending a statement. At such time better understanding may be gained by a different translation. Such is the case of Philippians 4:6. The AKJ uses the expression, "Be careful for nothing..." The word "careful" means being "full of care." Its meaning is better understood by our current word "anxious." The New King James reads, "Be anxious for nothing, but in everything by prayer and supplication, with thanksgiving, let your requests be made known to God." Prayer is a cure for anxiety.

There are two things about which we should never worry. One, don't ever worry about something that needs to be changed which you can change. To worry about it would delay constructively changing it. Second, never worry about something that needs to be changed and you can't change it. To worry about it won't change it. The way to handle such situations is to assess them carefully and acknowledge, "I can't change this thing which needs to be changed. I don't have the ability nor the authority to change it. God alone has the ability and authority to change it. Therefore, I will intrust it to the only One with both the ability and authority to change it. I resign the case and turn it over to the Lord." Once this is done the release afforded by the therapy of prayer is at work and anxiety begins to subside. It is the process of transferral of responsibility to the proper authority. This is not shirking a responsibility; it is submission to authority.

Peter, like David before him, exhorts believers to engage in "Casting all your care upon him; for he careth for you" (I Peter 5:7). The expression "he careth for you" means He is perpetually attending to us and our needs; He is not indifferent to your circumstances. While in the crucible of crisis, David experienced this care and advised: "Cast thy burden upon the Lord, and he shall sustain thee... (Psalm 55:22).

This "casting" is a decisive act of the will to be done prayerfully in obedience to God's Word. When it is truly done, a moment of release is experienced resulting in restoration. When the will engages in this "casting," multi-dimensional renewal is the consequence. The body relaxes, the mind is at peace, the spirit regains joy, and emotions are calmed.

FEAR

In "The Rime of the Ancient Mariner", Coleridge spoke descriptively of fear:

"Fear at my heart, as at a cup,

My life-blood seemed to sip!"

Fear drains life of energy. It not only depletes us physically, but it defeats us spiritually. It is a visionary vampire that drains life of meaning.

There is an antidote. There are Biblical principles which can be enacted through prayer. Start at the point of origin. "For God has not given us a spirit of fear; but of power, and of love, and of a sound mind" (II Timothy 1:7). When you have an abnormal fear, know its source. It is not of the Lord. Therefore, resolve with David, "what time I am afraid, I will trust in thee" (Psalms 56:3).

Prayerfully do as instructed in Psalms 91:2: "I will say of the Lord, He is my refuge and my fortress: my God; in him will I trust."

Trust in the Lord is the javelin thrust that defeats fear. Confidently you can relax knowing, "The Lord is good, a strong hold in the day of trouble; and he knoweth them that trust in him" (Nahum 1:7). Trust, faith, and belief are words which speak of the same thing. They speak of confidence in God's character.

When fear grips your life, pause, withdraw, and endeavor to relax physically. Then fix your mind on texts such as these. Acknowledge to God you believe His Word is as good as He and that you claim the provisions of these texts. Lovingly remind the Lord of His Word just as though He might have forgotten it. You can be assured He hasn't. For example, remind the Lord He said of persons such as you who plead for His help: "He shall call upon me, and I will answer him: I will be with him in trouble; I will deliver him, and honor him" (Psalms 91:14).

Interestingly converging stories from our space program dramatize the calming effect of prayer. Moments before blast off are tense. Fear and apprehension have a tendency to rise. Several Christian astronauts have told of becoming aware of their fear and praying. Monitors have recorded that at times corresponding with these prayers there has been a marked decrease in the blood pressure and pulse rate. Thus, the calming effects of prayer abating fear have been monitored.

"I just had a sense of peace about it..." is an expression I have heard many times from persons who have paused to pray amid fear. By tuning into the heavenly frequency peace has been obtained. Prayer makes us aware of our spiritual resources. An awareness of spiritual resources gives confidence and courage.

Take as your own the words of the Psalmist and pray aloud, "What time I am afraid, I will trust in thee. In God will I praise his word, in God I have put my trust; I will not fear what flesh can do unto me" (Psalm 56:3,4).

Such prayer enabled William Wordsworth, the great English poet, to speak of solitude in God's presence. "And I have felt a presence that disturbs me with the joy of elevated thought."

LONELINESS

You may sometimes feel like the main character in "The Fall" by Camus: "I have no friends; I have nothing but accomplices."

Dr. Abraham Maslow, famed research analyst, pessimistically concluded after his study of U.S. citizens: "The truth is that the average American does not have a real friend in the world." Does your life seem to be a living summary of that depressing statement?

Every effort is made to synthetically avoid loneliness. Crowds are sought by frequenting malls. Contact is perpetuated by being plugged into some listening device most of the time. Our fear of being alone only adds to our sense of loneliness. Our search for synthetic substitutes for fellowship only drives us further from the One who can provide for us in our loneliness.

Loneliness is two dimensional as evidenced by Christ in Gethsemane when He said to His disciples, "Sit here while I go and pray" (Matthew 26:36). The agony of the hour prompted Him to express a desire for fellowship with God the Father and man. He wanted His disciples to "sit" with Him while He addressed the Father in prayer. This evidences a deep need for dual companionship. Christ's loneliness was precipitated by rejection by many and a failure by others to understand His mission. It drove Him to seek dual fellowship. His loneliness was neither weak nor sinful.

Loneliness can result from the absence of one or both of these forms of companionship. We are instructed: "Set your affection on things above, not on things on the earth" (Colossians 3:2). What do you think is the primary object of most people's affection? Would it not be either persons, places, or things? A friend, children, a spouse, a girl or boy friend, a teammate, or a working associate may be your closest companion. It is good to develop a support system and to participate as a part of the support system of others. Places such as a residence, a retreat, or a club become dear to us. Things occupy much of our interest. We are gadget-oriented. Cars, boats, planes, videos, and the list of things absorbing our attention goes on.

When something happens to one of these things, we get lonely. Let a friend die, a house burn, or a car wreck and persons have a tendency to fall apart. Loneliness results. This can be so acute that it causes depression. Why? Because the person has had his or her affections set on things of earth and not things above. They complicate this by assuming the loneliness is a result of something missing in their lives that was there. The false assumption is that it is one of the earthly things. Actually that loneliness is a longing for the Lord. Only when the person who is designed and directed to set his or her affections on things above does so is that loneliness fulfilled.

When this is realized and the person starts spending time in prayer alone with the Lord, then and only then will loneliness be satisfied. It is a calling of the Spirit of God to the spirit of man. An open channel of prayer fulfills the loneliness. When viewed in this light, loneliness is seen as a friend calling us to set our affections on things above. It is a reminder that we have improperly invested our affection in things on earth.

An emptiness exists in many lives because they have neglected their companionship with the Lord. They may enjoy great prosperity and popularity and still feel lonely. The reason is prayer has been neglected. Often only the removal of a earthly object of affection will result in the redirection of love to the Lord.

Augustine's often-quoted truth calls us to fellowship with the Father through prayer. Augustine wrote, "Thou madest us for thyself, and our heart is restless, until it repose in thee."

In The Possessed, Kiriloff expressed the same thought in these words: "All my life I have been haunted by God." Relentlessly God pursues us in love. Our loving response to Him enriches life and spares us loneliness.

A solution for loneliness is to reach up to God for help and reach out to help others. Windows open outward as well as upward.

THERAPEUTIC TECHNIQUES
Use these strategic steps to spiritual healing of your body,

soul, and spirit:

* Meditate on God. Set aside a time each day to be very still and quiet. Fix your mind on the Lord Jesus Christ. This will condition you to be spiritually open and receptive to the Lord.

* Talk to the Lord out-loud. Use your own simple language. You need not be stilted or pious. Pour out your heart to God just as though He were not aware of your condition. He'll understand.

* Acknowledge God's blessings. Don't make every prayer time simply a time when you ask, seek, and knock. Affirm His blessings in your life. An attitude of gratitude is uplifting.

* Pray believing. Acknowledge to God and yourself that you believe He can work to supply your need and guide your life. Encompass your loved ones in this circle of love.

* Pray in positive terms. Neither you nor God needs to hear only a negative approach to life. What you are praying about might be gloom and doom but be positive about it.

* Cast your burden on Him. Don't loan Him your problems, give them to Him. Ask Him to enable you to do your best and trust Him to do His part.

* Pray for your enemies. Always pray the best for those who despise you, persecute you, and say false evil things about you. This will remove the primary blockage to your prayer life in most instances.

* Pray for others often. This will enable you to get your mind off yourself and yourself off your mind. Make a list of those for whom you should pray. In this way you can minister to others.

* Practice "breathing a prayer." Designated time for prayer is an expedient, but so is the practice of praying during idle moments during the day. Make a mini-chapel of your mind and retreat there at intervals during the day. This will re-fix your will on Christ.

* Continuously express a willingness to accept God's will. Imagine your prayer as being written. Conceive of the expression "Thy will be done" as a red highlighter. In concluding your prayer, highlight every word in red.

God doesn't always answer every petition, but He does always answer every person.

A skilled physical therapist can do a convalescent no good unless allowed to use known therapeutic techniques. Likewise, all we know of prayer is of little value unless we implement it. Take a moment to go to the school of prayer therapy by reviewing the techniques just noted. Now go over them again and assess how and when you are going to start employing each of them on a regular basis. When you consider what there is to gain, action seems all the more logical. The beginning of recovery and restoration is just a prayer away.

When the mind is weary, prayer does not increase the burden.

When emotions are frayed, prayer does not magnify the strain.

When the spirit is faint, prayer does not add to the trial.

An interview with the King of Kings can restore the soul.

From another century and an unknown origin comes this ancient benediction translated into the first person that is worthy of praying often:

"May the Lord Jesus Christ, who is the Splendor of the eternal Light, remove from my heart the darkness of night.

May He drive far from me the snares of the crafty enemy, and ever set to guard me the Angel of light.

That I may rise to His morning praises, kept safe in Him, in whom consists all the fullness of salvation.

May the Lord bless me, and protect me in His own Right Hand.

May He deliver me from all temptations of this life, and

pour the grace of His Holy Spirit into my heart.

May He take away from me every stain of sin, and lead me to the splendor of all His Saints.

May the Lord our God hear me, and favorably look on every one who calls to Him in need.

May He graciously grant the solace which human weakness needs, and avert the sins which oppose me.

And may He ever grant us all things profitable, both for our souls and bodies.

May the Almighty bless me from on high.

May He look upon my labor with favorable countenance, and hear your petitions with a pitying ear.

May He make my work well pleasing to Himself, and preserve my life in holiness and peace. Amen."

Prayer turns the dirge of half-beaten people into a march of conquerors. Don't let this therapy go unapplied.

The only time prayer fails is when we cease to pray.

7
WHY DOES GOD SAY "YES" OR "NO" TO MY PRAYERS?

Excessive heat and prolonged drought had combined to form formidable forceps with a grip on the southeast. Vegetation suffered as the dry earth depleted the roots and heat withered the shoots of the plants. Irritability ran at a record high among the population. Anxiety grew as each day brought record temperatures and no indication of rain.

The state of Georgia alone risked losing over $100,000,000 in crops and cattle. Our governor called on Monday asking me to review a proclamation he wanted to release calling for prayer. It was a letter-perfect expression of his spiritual desire.

Having been out of the state most of the week, I returned on Friday to find another call had come in from the governor. Upon calling him back he said, "The press has picked up on the idea of the prayer proclamation and will be following me around this weekend. Do you mind if I bring them to church with me?" Happily I replied, "Not at all. They need the preaching, and I need the practice."

Sunday came and with it the governor, his family, and TV representatives from CBS, NBC, ABC, and WTBS. The clear sky did not hint of betraying the forecast of no rain for the week.

Following inspiring music I read and made commentary on II Chronicles 7:14 which makes this challenging offer to God's people: "If my people, which are called by my name, shall humble themselves, and pray, and seek my face, and turn from their wicked ways; then will I hear from heaven, and will forgive their sin, and will heal their land."

Our congregation was then exhorted to get on our knees and express their humble confession to and contrition before God. It was a time of spiritual cleansing. This prayer time ended with no request for rain made of God. A brief explanation followed regarding us having done what our Lord requires regarding seeking God's forgiveness. Now, back to our knees we went to call on the Lord asking for rain.

After the service, I spent about thirty minutes greeting people before going outside. Cars had virtually vacated the near-empty parking lot. Members of the press were beginning to put away their equipment. Some lingered to chat about the prayer time.

Just then a sudden change in the velocity and temperature of the wind was accompanied by the strange, low rumble of thunder. Looking to the west an ominous black cloud moved over the hillside. Cameramen scurried to unload their equipment and set it up to get a shot of this unusual phenomenon.

Within fifteen minutes a gentle rain began to fall. As one of the reporters ran past me she said, "Can you believe this?" With joy, I replied, "Why, yes, I rather expected it."

Suddenly, we were forced to seek shelter as a two-inch down-pour flooded the area.

Monday through Wednesday nights a local television station carried a segment as part of the news which posed the question: "Was the rain an act of nature or a divine response to prayer?" Wednesday night's concluding segment resolved it was an act of God. Right!

That day the drought was broken and agricultural disaster avoided. God had kept His Word as He always does. II Chronicles 7:14 had been applied and He complied.

The story was carried internationally. Correspondence was received from such diverse places as Alaska, Saudi Arabia, Germany, and Japan. God had chosen to use the occasion of the humble prayer of His people to glorify Himself.

With joy I could join the Psalmist in saying, "I love the Lord, because He had heard my voice and my supplication" (Psalms 116:1).

Does God always answer prayer so immediately and directly?

My Dad and I had always been close. His retirement was going to give me the opportunity to do something significant and pleasing for him. I had just finished refurbishing a small lake-side cottage in the North Georgia mountains and was awaiting his visit the next day. It was going to be a holiday like he had dreamed and spoken of so often.

About noon I got a phone call: "Your Dad has had an abnormal abdominal attack and has been hospitalized. He won't be able to come visit you. His condition is undetermined."

A subsequent call informed us surgery was imminent. We began to pray for him to live. By all logic he should have lived. It was a small town hospital and the medical care wasn't the best. Complications developed immediately. Friends joined us in praying.

Then came the shock of a call which brought the grievous news, "I regret to tell you, your Dad just died."

"Why, God, why?"

Have you ever heard that prayer? Have you ever prayed it? Has your mind ever had to walk through the maze of confusion associated with an earnest prayer unanswered?

God answered that prayer. As always, His answer was determined by two things. One, His love. Two, His knowledge. His love is greater than ours and His knowledge fuller. They combine to forge His will which is always best.

Why He answered with a "no" must be interpreted in light of those two things. To have willed the delay of his exodus, even for a delightful North Georgia fishing trip, would have been to rob him of the splendor of the Father's house. Therefore, to have resented my Dad's going would have been to resist the blessings he had coming.

How does God answer prayer?

Often it is an immediate, positive response He grants. Frequently it is a delayed "yes." These responses are always thrilling. They are worth reporting for the glory of the Lord and as confidence builders to encourage prayer. When such a response is forthcoming, give glory to God. Don't jest in the person praying or even the process of prayer.

These are mere instruments for the Lord's use. His is the "kingdom, the power, and the glory."

Sometimes God answers "no." Whoever said "no" isn't an answer? If a child asks a parent to go to a certain event and the parent says no, the child knows an answer was given. Have you lived long enough to have learned to praise the Lord for the prayers He in love and wisdom said "no" to?

After a prayer meeting recently a young businessman said, "Pastor, you know the job I asked you to pray with me about? I didn't get it, and I thank God He was so loving as to say no to my request. The person who got it was transferred out of state and a month later the job discontinued. Thank God He said no."

If we had a good memory and were honest, we could recall many instances when a negative response to our prayer was a bigger blessing than a yes would have been.

God surely has a sense of humor or he never would have made a creature like homosapiens. In light of His sense of humor, I am sure sometimes He must answer, "You have got to be kidding!" Some of our prayers must make Him chortle. Have you ever paused to reflect on how silly some of your prayers have been? Sometimes selfish, often ridiculous, but rarely without a touch of irony.

With His sense of humor still active He must at times want to ask, "Wait just a minute! Which one of us is God?" Remember prayer is a request, not a dictum. God is not a divine bellman awaiting our command. It is He Who is God.

Sometimes God in love responds by saying, "Wait a while." These are often the best answers. I said best, not the most preferred. However, they being the best they should be received with praise. If we want what we want more than we want Him, we don't like this kind of answer. If we want Him more than the "thing" requested, we soon learn that a delay draws us closer to the One of Whom the request is made. This in itself brings joy.

Jesus Christ said, "Whatever things you ask when you pray, believe that you receive them, and you will have them" (Mark 11: 24).

Is that all there is to getting a prayer answered? No!

That is only one of several Biblical requirements for a productive prayer-life. Many individuals are disappointed in prayer simply because they know one or two requirements for proper prayer and, upon qualifying on those, think they have carte blanche opening to heaven. Though they comply with the few known requirements, they may be blind to a number of points at which they are not properly related to the Lord in order to have a vital prayer-life. Requirements for a good prayer-life are many-faceted. It is imperative that the person praying meet all of them.

Let's analyze our prayers. In doing so perhaps we will see that God has sometimes not answered a prayer when we thought He had.

Consider these CLASSIFICATIONS of prayer.

Every prayer is divided into two parts.

A. REQUEST. This may be made verbally or mentally. It is the thing for which a person asks.

B. REASON. For what reason has the request been made?

The request may be for $10,000,000.00. For what reason would you request such a sum? Reason one, might be in order to give it to the cause of Christ to help advance a specific ministry. Reason number two, might be in order to buy a mansion in which to live sensuously on drugs and serve Satan. The same request made by two different persons may have an entirely different reason behind it.

To God our reason is often more important than our request. In light of this the Lord might respond to requests in one of four ways. He might say - - -

REQUEST - YES == REASON - NO.
REQUEST - NO == REASON - YES.
REQUEST - YES == REASON - YES.
REQUEST - NO == REASON - NO.

More than a century ago an anonymous Confederate soldier penned words demonstrating the difference in a request and a reason.

"I asked God for strength, that I might achieve --
I was made weak, that I might learn humbly to obey.
I asked for help that I might do great things --

I was given infirmity, that I might do better things.
I asked for riches, that I might be happy --
I was given poverty, that I might be wise.
I asked for all things, that I might enjoy life --
I was given life, that I might enjoy all things.
I got nothing that I asked for --
but everything I had hoped for.
Despite myself, my prayers were answered,
I am, among all men, most richly blessed!"

Let's study some Biblical examples of each. Think of your own prayers as we review these segments of God's Word.

CLASSIFICATION # 1 REQUEST "YES" AND REASON "NO"

This example is extracted from the life of ancient Israel. God had blessed them by delivering them from slavery. During their 40 years of discipline in the wilderness God had fed them on manna. Whatever it was, it was a perfectly-balanced dietary substitute provided by God. The people began to complain about it and mumble for meat. Their spiritual discontent was improperly interpreted by them to be a desire for meat. It was really a hunger of their souls for fellowship with God.

Their REQUEST was for meat. Their REASON was a hunger of soul not body.

God said OK you will get your request but your reason is faulty. He sent them a covey of quail two miles wide and forty miles long. The least any person gathered was sixty-five bushels (Numbers 11: 31 - 33). They got what they requested. Their obstinate dissatisfaction evoked the wrath of God and while the meat was still in their teeth God began His discipline of them. Psalms 106: 13 - 15 reports the result: "And he gave them their request; but sent leanness into their soul." Their spiritual hunger, which they misinterpreted as physical hunger, remained. Thus, regarding their reason, God said no.

CLASSIFICATION # 2 REQUEST "NO" AND REASON "YES"

Abraham made a request that Sodom and Gomorrah not be destroyed (Gen. 18). The reason was so Lot and his family who lived there would not be killed. Abraham tried to bargain with God. He asked God not to destroy the city if 45 righteous people could be found in it (Vs. 28). God consented. Abraham lowered the total to 40 (Vs. 29). Again God conceded. Abraham bargained further for 35 (Vs. 30). God complied. Abraham persisted, "How about 20?" (Vs. 31). God acquiesced. Abraham counted up his own relatives in the city. There were Lot and his wife, two; two unmarried daughters, four; three married daughters and their husbands. They numbered ten. He made his final pitch, "Would you believe 10?" Agreed!

However, only Lot and his two unmarried daughters were believers. Thus, the cities were destroyed. The request was denied, but his reason was fulfilled. Lot and his family were saved.

A second example of REQUEST "NO" and REASON "YES" is found in II Cor. 12: 7. Paul made a request for his "thorn in the flesh" to be removed. His reason was that God might be glorified. The request was denied; the thorn remained. The reason was fulfilled; its presence glorified God.

God has concealed from us what the "thorn" was. It was something that caused Paul much misery. It was so painful physically or spiritually or both that he thought it was an impediment to God being glorified in his life. He was impressed that its removal would glorify God. Instead that "thorn" to this day is a hallmark of God's grace in Paul's life. It was the thing that has perhaps glorified God most in his life.

When we engage in prevailing prayer for our "thorn" to be removed and it isn't, there is a reason. It is an occasion for the grace of God to be manifest. There are occasions when we have difficulty discerning between our desire and God's will.

For example, it is only natural for a person to want to be healed of any sickness. It is appropriate to request healing but to cap the prayer with the pathos of Gethsamene, "Thy will be done." If healing doesn't come, our reaction should not be despair born of a defeatist attitude. Instead it should be like Paul who responded to the remaining thorn by saying, "I rather glory in my infirmities, in reproaches, in necessities, in persecutions, in distresses for Christ's sake: for when I am weak, then am I strong" (II Cor. 12: 9, 10).

Make sure your reason for requesting the removal of the "thorn" is not simply in order to have a bed of thornless roses.

CLASSIFICATION # 3 REQUEST "YES" AND REASON "YES"

Three men reached the final day of their earthly pilgrimage. Together they hung on separate crosses on Calvary. Suspended on the brink of eternity one found it not to be a time for final delusion. The one on the left hanging on the rim of hell willfully consigned himself to an eternal destiny apart from the love of God. In derision he cried out against Christ who was suspended on the center cross. Christ did not answer him. On the right hung a man equally guilty whose eyes were on the blood stained Savior. This was not to be his moment of condemnation but his commencement. The anguish of his soul took precedent over the suffering of his body. In his torment he called out to Christ, "Lord, remember me when thou comest into thy kingdom" (Luke 23: 42).

Both men were justifiably condemned. One changed his attitude as evidenced by him applying the title "Lord" to Jesus. He recognized Christ's deity. This poor, dumb thief realized something a lot of people fail to comprehend. He knew Jesus was Lord or a liar, and he believed Jesus. Application of this title reveals his reason for the request which was to follow. It indicated he wanted to be forgiven of his sins; to be saved.

His request was to be remembered by Christ when He came into His kingdom. His reason was he wanted salvation.

His request was granted. Jesus said, "Today shall you be with me in Paradise." The reason he would be in Paradise was he was then and there saved.

A second classic example of a yes answer being given to both request and reason is found in John 11. Jesus had delayed His coming to the home of Mary and Martha when told Lazarus, their brother, was critically ill. Lazarus died before Christ arrived. His grieving sisters in their confusion chastened Christ for not coming sooner. The mood was depressing, mournful. Jesus prayed a prayer containing a request and revealing His reason.

His request was for Lazarus to come forth (Vs. 43).

His reason was "that they might believe" (Vs. 42).

Lazarus obediently came forth; the dead man lived.

As a result, many "believed on him" (Vs. 45). Those spiritually dead came alive. They formed the nucleus responsible for assembling the large Palm Sunday crowd that greeted Christ.

We tend to think that only when we get a "yes - yes" response to a prayer that it has been answered. We need to rethink what constitutes an answered prayer.

CLASSIFICATION # 4 REQUEST "NO" AND REASON "NO"

Little things can cause big power failures. NASA space scientists say the slightest piece of lint or the residual moisture from a finger print can cause a sophisticated missile to go off target. Such a slight thing out of place can result in missing the intended goal. The balance of elements is even more critical in prayer.

There are several causes for both our request and reason being denied. All are on our end of the line. Therefore, if you don't have a good prayer life, check the reason or reasons. They are within you. Consider these and apply them to your life.

1. Failure to exercise faith in prayer - Matthew 21:22

"And all things, whatsoever ye ask in prayer, believing, ye shall receive."

"Believing" is simply having genuine trust in God; faith. In this instance it is God's will we are to trust. Some try to make it faith in faith, and others faith in prayer. Neither is the object of our belief; God is.

Proverbially, we are urged to "Trust in the Lord with all thine heart; and lean not unto thine own understanding" (Proverbs 3:5). The Hebrew word translated "trust" was a wrestler's term.

It meant to grab a hold on and not let go. It was used as a "body slam." If you "trust" in the Lord you will grab hold of Him and not let go regardless of circumstances. In this text YAHWEH is the name used for and translated "God." It was His name used in conjunction with His covenant promises. This is an appeal to trust the God who keeps His promises.

We cannot honor God more than by believing what He says. Alexander the Great had a famous and trusted philosopher in his court who was a pauper. The poor man appealed to Alexander for aid. Gladly the conqueror of the known world gave him a letter allowing him to receive what he wished from his treasury. His request for the large sum of ten thousand pounds was resented by the treasurer who thought it too large a sum. The treasurer reported it to Alexander who replied, "Let the money be instantly paid. I am delighted with the philosopher's way of thinking; he has done me a singular honor; by the largeness of his request he shows the high idea he has conceived both of my superior wealth and my royal munificence." Do we show comparable confidence in our God?

It was said of Israel as they approached the land of promise, "They could not enter because of unbelief." The same can be said of the inadmissibility of many of our prayers.

2. Selfishness - James 4: 2, 3

"...ye have not, because ye ask not. Ye ask, and receive not, because ye ask amiss, that ye may consume it to your lusts."

Wouldn't it be grievous to check into heaven and have the Lord ask, "Why didn't you let me bless you more? All you had to do was ask." There may be many blessings missing from life, but don't let it be because you failed to ask.

Are there areas of your life you fail to pray about? Are there issues you never address with the Lord? Could that be, in part, why these things haven't gone well?

Most persons are more bewildered by the request made without a visible answer forthcoming. Again, the reason for asking is the critical issue. In this instance the request might be good but the reason isn't. Some requests aren't granted simply because they are motivated by an unacceptable desire. God doesn't parcel out goodies simply to appease our improper appetites. He is not in the business of providing our inordinate desires. Self-gratification is not aided by God. There is no way to get the gratification from evil imagined; not even by prayer. In effect, such an attitude was first expressed in Eden where the essence of the prayer of Adam and Eve would have been, "Not your will, but ours be done." It didn't work then, and it doesn't work now. In another garden, Gethsamene, the second Adam prayed as we must, "Not my will, but thy will be done."

A sure way to avoid letting your own lust color your prayers is recorded by the Psalmist: "Delight thyself also in the Lord; and he shall give thee the desires of thine heart" (37:4). When you get to where you enjoy pleasing the Lord more than yourself then His will takes supersedence in your life. He delights to do His will. When it is the desire of your heart you will have it. The point at which His will and your desire converge is the parade ground of victory.

John Calvin said, "James meant briefly this -- that our desires ought to be bridled; and the way of bridling them is to subject them to the will of God."

3. Carnality - Psalms 66: 18

"If I regard iniquity in my heart, the Lord will not hear me."

Make certain you do not have secret sympathy for sin. Don't expect God to tolerate sin simply because you coddle it. If we pretend to be what we are not, the Lord Adonai, my Support, my Help, will not play along with us and confirm our pretense by answering our prayer. There is no double dealing with God. The heart that is heard is the one weary of sin and longing to be delivered from it. The frailest of prayers from a clean heart is heard. John Calvin said, "Integrity of heart is indispensable." Indulgence of iniquity bars the door of prayer.

"Iniquity" is any violation of God's will. It is a punishable offense against God's holiness and authority. One major punishment is unanswered prayer. This indicates why sin is so serious. It blocks the prayer channel. Confession clears it.

4. Lack of compassion - Proverbs 21: 13

"Whosoever stoppeth his ears at the cry of the poor, he also will cry himself, but shall not be heard."

There may on occasion be good reason for not giving to the poor, but insensitivity is never one. Having a hard-heart toward those in distress causes God to show no pity toward those having no sympathy. It was for this reason God was inattentive to the prayers and fasting of a multitude in ancient Israel (Isaiah 50). It is worse to be greedy than it is to be needy. In no place does God condemn need though He does greed. Those showing no interest in the needs of others are spiritually bankrupt. Their poverty of compassion is worse than poverty of capitol. It results in the heavenly prayer bank being closed. Conversely, "God loveth a cheerful giver" (II Cor. 9:7).

5. Lack of domestic tranquility - I Peter 3: 7c
"...that your prayers be not hindered."
In I Peter 3 the husband/wife relationship is defined in the first seven verses. In the first six verses the wife is told to be submissive, faithful, not a nagger, chaste, and beautiful inside. The husband is exhorted to be understanding and recognize his wife to be his equal spiritually. Because of this he should plan with her, converse with her as his peer, hold her in high regard as knowledge would demand, and relate to her in love. Failure to fulfill these roles amounts to insurrection against the will of God. A disrupted relationship with the Father consequences.

Disharmony between a husband and wife results in disunion in prayer. Scripture appeals for a harmonious relationship between husband and wife. They being an example of Christ's relationship with His church should typify love.

Sometimes one partner in a marriage relationship gets out of fellowship with the Lord and might even try to break the marriage contract. That does not mean the other partner's prayer life is disrupted also. If the non-offending partner has the right attitude toward the alienating mate, his or her prayer life is still effective. Though the circumstances may be beyond the person's control, their own attitude isn't.

The essence of this passage is that if you are out of fellowship with your mate because of wrongdoing on your part, you are out of fellowship with the Father and therefore your prayers are not heard. You must get right with one another before you can get through with the Father.

6. Pride - Job 35: 12, 13
"There they cry, but none giveth answer, because of the pride of evil men. Surely God will not hear vanity, neither will the Almighty regard it."

If pride turns a person's head he is looking the wrong way. A guaranteed way to have God for an opponent is to have improper pride. The record declares: "God resisteth the proud, but giveth grace to the humble" (James 4: 6).

There are two kinds of pride. One is good and the other bad. The good kind makes a person ashamed not to be and do his or her best. This kind is a marvelous motivating force. This kind of pride should permeate our prayers. Opposite of this is the bad kind; that which is egocentric, self centered, selfish. Vanity is a mirror image of pride. This kind is always wrong. The Bible gives no complete catalogue listing of all sins. However, every time there is a grouping of sins listed pride is mentioned first. A prideful person is not prone to pray. Prayer is stimulated by gratitude, love for another, submissiveness, dependance, and reliance. These traits are absent from an inflated ego. The type person who can strut sitting down is not likely to kneel. A matchless example of a person praying with improper pride was cited by Christ. With public pride he "prayed thus with himself, God, I thank thee, that I am not as other men are..." (Luke 18: 11). This man, though pretentiously addressing God, was actually talking to himself; congratulating himself. The expression "prayed thus with himself" means he directed his prayer to himself. He must have been the first to write the nursery rhyme with the line "what a good boy am I."

Jesus concluded this narrative by saying, "...everyone that exalteth himself shall be abased; and he that humbleth himself shall be exalted" (Luke 18: 14).

7. Lack of obedience - I John 3: 22

"And whatsoever we ask, we receive of Him, because we keep His commandments, and do those things that are pleasing in his sight."

If we are disobedient to His revealed will there is no need to pray for more of His will to be revealed in order to be disobedient to it also. Do what you know to do before you ask for more to do. When He observes a willing spirit and obedient nature

He delights to reveal more for the person to do.

We are often like a child that comes to its mother with a hand behind his back asking for more cookies. The mother insists on seeing what is in the concealed hand. When finally it is reluctantly displayed, it is full of cookies. Mother then says, "Eat the cookies you have and I will give you more."

Obey the orders given before asking for more orders. It is the faithful and obedient who are given further and fuller revelation. Pre-commitment to His will, even before knowing it, is a good way to get to know it. He delights to let a person know what to do who has pre-prayed "Thy will be done." That doesn't hint of resignation. It shouts of resolution.

8. Failure to be in fellowship - Ephesians 6: 18

"Praying always with all prayer and supplication in the Spirit, and watching thereunto with all perseverance and supplication for all saints."

Praying "in the Spirit" results from deep intimacy with the Lord. It is in effect prayer issuing from a believer who is given by the Holy Spirit a great sense of urgency about what to pray. Sensitivity growing out of fellowship with the Lord enables the Spirit to impress the pray-er with what needs to be prayed. It is the Holy Spirit teaching us what to share with the Father in the name of the Son. This is prayer that has God as its object and origin.

We, like Christian in Pilgrim's Progress, have been given the weapon of "All-prayer." He used it in his moment of greatest need in the Valley of the Shadow against the fiends which attacked him. His fervent prayer stopped their advance and resulted in them being routed. To go into spiritual warfare without the weapon of prayer sharpened by close fellowship with the Lord is to fight with a paper sword.

Sin breaks our fellowship, not our relationship, with the Lord. Cleansing results in renewal of fellowship. To try to pray while out of fellowship is comparable to trying to drive down a road without removing a major blockade. Confession removes the blockade of sin. Our willingness to confess evidences to the Lord our love for Him and a desire not to be separated from Him. It is an act of obedience indicating He has first place in our life.

9. Failure to comply with God's will - I John 5:14, 15

"And this is the confidence that we have in him, that, if we ask anything according to his will, he heareth us: And if we know that he hears us, whatsoever we ask, we know that we have the petitions that we desire of him."

"In His will is our peace," said Dante.

Finding God's will is often challenging. Frequently it is as easy as opening the Bible. In many instances He has stated His will clearly and emphatically. However, having given us His Word as a basis for guidance He then created us with a mind with which to reason and discern. Using these two tools we have to seek His will in many areas not directly addressed. When His will is known prayer is then simple. It is merely a matter of saying, "Thy will be done." This is when superimposition of His will on ours becomes a blessing.

There are times when after seeking His will through prayer I have resorted to praying: "Lord in light of my love for You and based on the knowledge I now have I am committing myself to this believing it to be your will. Please be merciful to me. If I am wrong it is out of my ignorance not my obstinance." In such an instance I think God reads the intent of the heart. In voicing such a prayer the heart is totally bent on God's will.

There are some things we don't need to pray about. That statement might seem to be unspiritual to some. We don't need to pray for things we know to be out of God's will. He is not going to war against Himself and do something contrary to His will just to oblige us. If it is against His will, it is contrary to

His will. For Him to grant a request contrary to His will would be to forfeit His very nature as God. For example, there is no need for a Christian considering marriage to a non-Christian to pray, "God if you don't shut the door I will know it is your will for us to get married." The door is already shut in II Corinthians 6: 14, "Be ye not unequally yoked together with unbelievers: for what fellowship hath righteousness with unrighteousness?" Prayer for the person's salvation should precede prayer for marriage.

Occasionally a person will say, "It seems like my prayers don't even reach the ceiling." That might be true. The implication, however, is that God is out of business. In reality they are out of sync with His will.

How is your prayer life? There is a way to eliminate the reason it isn't better. I John 1: 9 is the formula for removing hindrances to your prayer life: "If we confess our sins, he is faithful and just to forgive us our sins, and to cleanse us from all unrighteousness."

"If" means this action is optional. It does not imply there is an alternative way of getting the result, however. If a person chooses to have hindrances removed this is the only way.

"We" means it is personal; no one else can do it for you.

To "confess" means to agree with God about it and name it to Him as a sin for which we want forgiveness.

"He" and He alone will produce the desired result.

He is "faithful" to do it. This means He keeps His promises and will do it every time we confess.

By His justice it is meant He has provided an appropriate way to do it and maintain His holy nature.

"To forgive" means to remove it from the record. This is primarily a reference to initial salvation.

To "cleanse" from "unrighteousness" relates to forgiveness of sins of a Christian. In the New Testament, the prefix "un" before righteousness is a reference to the sins of a Christian. This cleansing opens the prayer channel.

You can enclose the Alps Mountains in an aspirin box easier than you can have your prayers answered without complying with this form of confessional prayer. You can put the Pacific Ocean in a Coke bottle easier than you can have a vital prayer life out of fellowship with the Lord. I John 1:9 should be memorized by every Christian. The precepts contained therein should be a regular part of daily prayer. Keep the prayer channel clean of little things and it is less likely to become blocked by big things.

8
KNOW WHAT YOU ARE SAYING
WHEN YOU ARE PRAYING

Rarely has there been a time when fewer people gave evidence of knowing "...what we should pray for as we ought..." (Romans 8:26). Praying "as we ought" means knowing what or what not to pray for, and knowing how to pray. Every generation, secular and spiritual, seems to have its cliches. These buzzwords or catch- phrases come and go with greater or lesser degrees of popularity. Often a phrase or word is lifted out of context and applied in a manner never intended. If such improper application is uncontested, it becomes not only vogue for a season but also a contamination of mainstream doctrine. In most instances the intent of the user is unimpeachable. Even if this is true and the teaching false, it needs to be addressed in love.

PRAYING A HEDGE OF THORNS
It is currently popular to "pray a hedge of thorns around" an individual or event. Many people use the expression thinking it to be Biblical, without knowing what it means.

It appears that by praying it persons are asking the Lord to protect a person. Truly that is a commendable intent. God understands the intent regardless of what phrase is used to voice it. However, it is best to use Bible phrases correctly and not to use near-Bible terms almost properly.

Apparently the expression is derived from an expression which occurs in Hosea 2:5-8 where it is stated, "I will hedge up the way with thorns, and make a wall..." In this historical narrative which is used to teach an important spiritual lesson, Gomer, the wife of Hosea is used as an illustration. She, a literal character, is used to depict ancient Israel and modern Christians. Her improper conduct can be summed up by saying she was "on the wrong path." So was Israel of that era. Many believers presently are found on that same inappropriate path. Being on the wrong path is a reference to going against God's will. The passage is a two-fold prophetic pronouncement against evil.

The expression "hedge up the way with thorns" speaks of the Lord acting in such a way as to guarantee the redirection of the life of Gomer/Israel/a believer out of fellowship. Notice the thorns are across the path, not around the person. The thorns are not used in this context to protect the person but to frustrate the person and cause futility in his or her life. It is a reference to unexpected hindrances put in a person's way--a disappointing impediment intended to stop a person from pursuing his or her own way. The thorns are not a defense for a Godly person but a deterrent from doing evil by a person acting in an ungodly manner.

"Praying a hedge of thorns" is not a magic formula. We are at no point encouraged to pray a hedge of thorns around a person. In Hosea's account thorns are across the path, not around the person. If we are going to use the term "thorns," we need to know what it was used to mean. To pray the term from a Biblical point of understanding means to ask God to cause despair in a person's life that is intended eventually to cause loyalty to

God's will. A good way to express this is to pray for a person to walk after God's own way, that is, to do God's will.

A closer observation reveals that Gomer, as Israel, endured the thorns or hindrances and walked the wrong path in sin for years. A second term was used in the text to refer to even more extreme frustrations. Remember Gomer is a picture of ancient Israel and modern believers who are not doing God's will. Her unfaithfulness is spoken of by saying she "has played the harlot" and "done shamefully" (verse 5). In order to purposefully frustrate her and bring her to repentance, God promised a greater restraint. It was said He would "wall her in." If little, irritating frustrations, comparable to thorns, don't work, God promises bigger ones analogous to a masonry wall in His effort to restore the person to the joy of salvation.

"Thorns" and "walls" are intended to help a person see "the way of the transgressor is hard," but "he that regardeth reproof shall be honored" (Proverbs 13:15,18). A previous generation would have prayed for the Lord to bring such people to their knees.

An experience in the life of ancient Israel was an occasion of God building a wall, an ultimate frustration. Israel had been delivered from Egyptian captivity. God had led them kicking and screaming toward the land of promise. All the way they had complained against God and criticized His appointed leaders.

Finally, figuratively God built a wall and said, "...they should not enter into my rest" (Psalms 95:11).

Why would God plant thorns and build walls? The answer must be understood in light of His wisdom and love. From His divine vantage point, He can see where the path leads and in love He does not want one traveling it to suffer the end result. As is true of all paths, even the wrong path has an end. For the person doing the wrong things on the wrong path, "the end of those things is death;" but for those on God's intended path, "the end is everlasting life" (Romans 6:21,22). Any temporary frustration that prevents the ultimate frustration is a good one.

A second occasion in which the term appears is in the life of Job. There Satan refers to God putting a hedge of protection around Job (Job 1:10). In this instance reference is to providing protection. Seeking God's protection is an essential.

Know what you are asking when praying for a hedge. Is it to hinder a person from doing evil or from what evil might do to a person?

BINDING SATAN

With sweet spirit and noble intent persons often pray "We bind Satan in this place." Wow!

This commendable desire is based on Christ's statement to Simon Peter. Christ had asked, "Whom do you say I am?" (Matthew 16:15). Peter's response was the classic testimony of Christ's nature and role. He said, "Thou are the Christ, the Son of the living God" (verse 16).

"Jesus answered and said unto him, 'Blessed art thou, Simon Bar-jonah: for flesh and blood hath not revealed it unto thee, but my Father which is in heaven. And I say also unto thee, That thou art Peter, and upon this rock I will build my church; and the gates of hell shall not prevail against it. And I will give unto thee the keys of the kingdom of heaven: and whatsoever thou shalt bind on earth shall be bound in heaven: and whatsoever thou shalt loose on earth shall be loosed in heaven'" (Matthew 16:17-19).

Hermeneutics is the science of interpreting Scripture in light of what it meant at the time of origin. Our application and understanding is aided by knowing what it meant to the persons involved. In this instance, what did this expression mean to Peter? He comprehended it in light of his understanding of the terms at the time used.

The setting was one of witnessing. At issue was "who was Jesus?" Peter gave the most complete answer recorded at the time. Then Jesus promised him "the keys of the kingdom of heaven." The holy scrolls were kept locked in a special cabinet. Only mature, well-schooled rabbis had the key to the cabinets in which were kept the Word of God. When a young rabbi completed his training, he was graduated by being given not a diploma but keys to the cabinet. He could unlock the cabinet, take out the word, and share it. If he didn't unlock the cabinet, the word was kept from the people.

Peter, like a young rabbi, had learned his lesson well. He knew and confessed who Christ was. He had finished the basic course and was now ready for post-graduate training. Jesus acknowledged he was "blessed" and on this his commencement He gave Peter "the keys." Knowing who Christ was Peter now had opportunity to bear witness.

In light of usage given these terms in his time Peter knew Christ to be saying, "Peter, if you don't 'unlock,' that is, take out the word and share it, but rather leave it bound by lock, not even the power of heaven can unloose it. If you don't bear witness of me, heaven has no witness it can give. If you do unlock, that is unbind it, heaven will unbind it in hearts and lives. If you 'bind' it on earth not even heaven can unlock, unbind, it. If, however, you do unlock it, the power of heaven will accompany the word."

In summary, the expression related to bearing witness of Christ had nothing to do with "binding Satan." Think a moment. If you had the power to bind Satan in a room, why not in a house? If you can bind him in a house, why not bind him in your city? If you can bind him in your city, wouldn't it be selfish not to bind him in your entire state? If in your state, why not your nation? If you have the ability to bind Satan in one nation, why not bind him in the whole world? It is a wonderful thought, but not in the realm of reality.

If that were possible, it would frustrate prophecy for Satan has been unloosed to work on earth presently. There is coming a glorious day when our beloved Lord will bind him and cast him into the lake of fire (Revelation 20:1,2,10). That is the happy ending. However, the ultimate binding has to be done by one greater than Satan. Satan, being the fourth most powerful supernatural being in the universe, cannot be bound by us, but he can easily be bound by our Beloved Jesus.

Use of the term "binding Satan" is improper. However, it expresses an ambition for his influence to be restricted and his desire unfulfilled in our life or an event. There are many commendable ways of praying for this. Jesus said one way is to pray "deliver us from evil" (Matthew 6:13).

A FRESH ANOINTING BY THE SPIRIT

With admirable ambition persons often pray "God give us a fresh anointing," or "anoint this service."

Evidently, what this most commonly expresses is a desire for God to work in a meaningful manner, to be in control. That is a splendid intent. More of us should share that yearning. However, again, such a prayer departs from what the Bible means by anointing.

Jesus said, "The Spirit of the Lord is upon me, because he hath anointed me..." (Luke 4:18). Who did the anointing and with what? This text is a quote from Isaiah 61:1. This is a verse translated from the Septuagint. The Septuagint was a New Testament translation of the Hebrew Old Testament into New Testament Greek. This is an accurate translation of the Septuagint and is not a violation of good translation techniques or grammar. However, by going back to the Hebrew text of Isaiah, this passage becomes clearer. There it is said "the Lord hath anointed me." Thus, God the Father anointed God the Son. Being in the instrumental case it means God the Father anointed God the Son with God the Holy Spirit. "Now he which establishes us with you in Christ, and hath anointed us, is God, who has also sealed us, and given the earnest of the Spirit in our hearts" (II Corinthians 1:21,22). The Holy Spirit does not anoint. He is the anointing. As "God anointed Jesus of Nazareth with the Holy Ghost", so the Father is the one who anoints believers, and it is the Holy Ghost with which He anoints. Therefore, don't pray that the Holy Spirit will anoint a person or service.

Anointing with the Spirit refers to the act of God the Father causing God the Holy Spirit to take up permanent residence in the believer. This anointing with the Spirit occurs at the moment of salvation. It is the basis of all His ministry to and in behalf of the believer.

Persons who want what is implied by praying for a fresh anointing should rather ask to be filled with the Holy Spirit. This is an expression meaning to be under the domination of Christ.

We Christians have a tendency to group ourselves around buzzwords and phrases. Often these camps disapprove of each other because they don't use the same terminology. Actually there are four ways of saying the same thing. "Being filled with the Spirit," "doing the will of God the Father," "letting Jesus be Lord," and "living according to the teachings of the Bible" all mean basically the same thing. Any one of these contains all that is intended by a prayer for anointing and is a better expression. Don't fault a person simply because they don't use your terms, if they are using Bible terms correctly.

WHEN TWO AGREE IN PRAYER
Jesus said, "...if two of you shall agree on earth as touching

any thing that they shall ask, it shall be done for them of my Father which is in heaven" (Matthew 18:19).

Misunderstanding of this truth has caused much disappointment. Many times Christians want a thing so badly that they convince themselves it is what God wants. They search for someone to agree with them and then think they have God in a corner. They have Him two to One. In their minds He has no option but to do what they have agreed He should do. When God does not do what they expect of Him, then disillusionment results.

Don't expect to use this verse to hold God hostage and demand as ransom the answer to some mutual self-delusion which is in reality only a human wish and not the divine will. God can't be bought off.

Self-delusion must not be confused as being God's will. Even if two agree they must be in agreement within the will of God. Prayers of agreement, like all others, must be postmarked "Thy will be done." It matters not how many sincere people agree--the veto rests with God. Collectively they must agree with Him. This promise is conditioned by the same requirement noted in the next verse for Christ to be where two or three are gathered. As the gathering must be "in His name," so must prayer be "in His name". To be "in His name" means to be of His nature and for His sake.

This promise does not amend all other requirements, provisions, and promises regarding prayer. It goes only so far as they go. That is sufficient, for they go the limit. It is within that limit that agreement must be reached. John 14:13,14 makes a similar promise; however, John 15:7 carefully adds a definitive statement. The persons agreeing must be spiritually united with Jesus and be keepers of His Word.

By using the multiple number two, an attempt is made to reduce the possibility of selfishness. However, selfishness cannot be eliminated by mathematics alone. An entire football team might agree to pray for a victory. Prayer that in effect results in the failure of someone else isn't birthed of love nor does it have selflessness for a midwife. Believers are to function as a community, not as individualists.

By using the smallest of multiple numbers, emphasis is placed on the fact that numbers alone don't determine God's will. They may well influence His will. They might well even enable His will to be done. They do not of themselves force God to respond as they desire.

The verb "agree" in the Greek text is SUMPHONEO. Our English word "symphony" can be heard in it. It was used of musical instruments which are different but when played together make a symphony of sound. The sounds agree even though they are not the same. For there to be music all instruments have to play as one under the direction of the "Conductor."

This text, like all others, is better understood in light of the teaching intended by its context. The passage deals with church discipline, not prayer. It does have a proper application to prayer, but relates principally to body-life. The two who are to agree are defined in verse 15. They are an offending brother and one offended. When both parties of an offense are led of the Holy Spirit to agree, that is, to be together symphonically, they can be assured heaven smiles on the agreement. Peaceful arbitration in disputes is of the Lord.

This may be a disappointing interpretation of the passage. However, an even greater blessing than initially anticipated emerges when disappointments are properly interpreted. Harmony within the church family, God's supernatural "orchestra", shows the "Conductor" is directing. That is a heavenly agreement.

If you apply the passage to prayer, be certain that "agreement" is only one factor you are depending upon to make the prayer acceptable to the Lord. All other requirements for answered prayer are still in force.

A PRAYER LANGUAGE

God reads the heart. He isn't picky about words for He knows the thought and intent of the heart. In spite of this a school of thought has emerged which advocates having a "prayer language" as a superior way to pray. Three primary texts are used to support this theory. One is Romans 8:26 which states: "Likewise the Spirit also helpeth our infirmities: for we know not what we should pray for as we ought: but the Spirit itself makes intercession for us with groaning which cannot be uttered." This they say is a reference to a prayer language. A careful observation of this passage reveals that it is the Spirit who makes the audible sounds. The Spirit Himself does the groaning, not the person praying. Also obvious is the fact that these sounds "cannot be uttered." Hence, if this were a reference to a prayer language, and it isn't, it would be for silent prayer only.

A second primary text used by advocates of a prayer language is I Corinthians 13:1 which states: "Though I speak with the tongues of men and angels..." Reputedly the prayer language is angelic language. A study of angel communication with human beings helps our understanding. What language did angels use when they spoke to humans?

When the shepherds heard angels praising God (Luke 2:13, 14) and when John heard the heavenly chorus (Revelation 4:8), no interpreters were necessary. Angels always spoke the language of the persons to whom they were speaking. Biblically there is no such thing as an unintelligible heavenly language. From the standpoint of Scripture, the concept of a prayer language is indefensible. Confused teaching on this subject has developed a group of experience-seekers. Not finding consistency in the practice, many have become disillusioned and frustrated. Thus, zealous persons with commendable intent have been defeated in what was promised to be a sweet victory.

One further text is often used by advocates of a prayer language. It is I Corinthians 14:2 which states: "For he that speaketh in an unknown tongue speaketh not unto men, but unto God..." It should be noted that the word "unknown" is in italics, meaning it wasn't in the original text. Earliest manuscripts know nothing of an "unknown tongue." Obviously the word "tongue" in Acts 2:4,6,8,11 were known languages recognized by listeners. The Holy Spirit enabled this miraculous communication in unlearned languages. Paul said, "I will pray with the spirit, and I will pray with the understanding also" (verse 15). He wanted to engage both in praying. Part of the harvest (fruit) of the Spirit noted in Galatians 5:22,23 is "self-control." To allegedly speak in an "unknown prayer language" would evidence having no self-control in the act. According to the Galatians text such conduct would not be authored by the Holy Spirit.

A simple question: "How can you 'ask' if the language you are alleged to be speaking is unknown?"

It is obvious that many do not find the Bible to teach the concept of a prayer language. However, if they are wrong and there is such a thing, and you don't have it, keep two things in mind. One, don't seek it. The Spirit gives gifts "as He wills." Second, don't feel inferior if you don't have a prayer language. Millions of mature dedicated believers through the centuries haven't had one either.

Don't complicate your prayer life. Use your own known language. It is not language that hinders prayer, but sin. Don't let what you don't have hinder what you do have. You have the right vocally or silently to come boldly before the throne of grace in the name of Jesus Christ. Having the right to do it and not doing it is little or no better than not having the right.

ANOINTING AND PRAYING FOR THE SICK

Tim stood beside the bed of his critically ill brother along with a well-intending group from another church that had come insisting that they be allowed to anoint him with oil and pray for him. Tim refused to allow them to anoint his comatose brother, but appealed to them to pray with him for his brother. There was no anointing. Many persons prayed for Tim's brother even though the doctors gave them no hope of his recovery. By God's grace he miraculously recovered.

Ralph was diagnosed as being terminally ill with cancer. Members of this same group insisted that they be allowed to anoint him and pray for him. They did so with a pure motive. Within four months Ralph died.

All persons involved acted with admirable intent. How does James 5:14,15 apply? It states, "Is any sick among you? Let him call for the elders of the church; and let them pray over him, anointing him with oil in the name of the Lord: And the prayer of faith shall save the sick, and the Lord shall raise him up..."

Is that a guaranteed formula for healing? If it is, it is a formula for perpetual life on this planet. By virtue of the fact no person has had endless life on planet earth, it obviously isn't an all-inclusive panacea. This is not a formula for canceling the sentence of death pronounced on the entire human race. To believe that it is would not be faith, but presumption. How then is this text to be understood?

All acts of God must be understood and all texts interpreted in light of (a) His love, and (b) His knowledge. He knows more and has greater love than we. He is too wise not to know what is best in every instance. He is too loving not to do what is best at all times. Why He heals some and not others must be understood in light of those two facts.

It is appropriate that every believer do all that the Lord expects in all things. This is particularly true in matters of healing. Based on the passage in James, two things are advocated: (a) anointing with oil, and (b) prayer. Just exactly what that means deserves study.

Before considering what these acts involve, consideration should be given the word translated "sick." In verse 14 it is the Greek verb ASTHENEO. It consists of the word STHENOS meaning "strength" with the prefix "A" meaning "negative." Thus, it means "without strength" and is often translated "feeble" or "weak." In verse 15 the verb translated "sick" is KAMNO primarily meaning to be "weary" from constant work. Though these words may refer to an illness, they do not always. Therefore, what is applicable here is not just pertinent to sickness.

In the Greek text there are two words which can be translated "anoint."

CHIRO, the root for "Christos" is one. "Christ" is the anglicized form of this word which means "the Anointed One." In the Old Testament era prophets, priests, and kings were anointed by putting oil on their brow. It was confined to sacred and symbolical anointing. "Jesus" was the name given to the Son of God who was given birth by the virgin Mary. Jesus was later given the title "Christ." This title identifies Him as the believer's Prophet, Priest, and King. As the anointing ceremony identified the persons set aside by the act, so this title designated Jesus' role.

ALEIPHO is the other word often translated "anoint." It is best understood if translated "oiling with oil." It described a process very much like modern day nurses rubbing a patient who has a fever with alcohol. It meant to massage or knead. The substance used was olive oil or an ointment. Rabbinical writings of the era speak of the healing properties of olive oil. It is still used medicinally in the orient. This is the word used to describe what the Good Samaritan did for the wounded man on the road to Jericho. It assuaged and mollified his wounds.

The word used by James was ALEIPHO. The text was interpreted to mean using the best medicine possible up until the 12th Century when the Roman Catholic Church changed its application. At that point they made anointing of various orifices by dabbing oil on them a sacrament; Extreme Unction. It should be noted this was a grave departure from what James taught. The sacrament is intended to prepare a person for death. James is teaching about healing. Unfortunately some protestant groups simplified this process and began putting oil on the forehead and praying for the sick.

The only other occasion of anointing the sick with oil and praying for them is recorded in Mark 6:13. It was the first time Christ sent out His disciples to minister. They anointed persons with oil though Christ did not instruct them to do so. On subsequent mission ventures they did not anoint with oil. However, the Greek word describing this anointing was the same root as ALEIPHO. It was not a ceremonial, symbolical, or sacramental act. The Mark passage confirms the James principle of oiling with oil, but is not a doctrinal passage as is James.

If persons are going to be literal they should not put oil on the brow, but massage the body with oil. If they want to keep the spirit of the passage they should do the two things advocated in the text: (a) use the best medicine available, and (b) pray. Once these have been done a person can be assured they have done all that God requires of them. Therefore, the result of the process is left in the hands of God. Remembering that His decisions are based on superior wisdom and love, the outcome, whatever it may be, must be interpreted in light of these factors. If the person is not healed, it is not because of a failure on behalf of the persons fulfilling their responsibilities.

James makes an urgent appeal for prayer. The entire process is to be initiated by the sick person, "...let him call..." This is to enable an evidence of faith.

Involved in that prayer should be repentant confession. In Psalms 86, the Psalmist appeals to the Lord with this statement: "Bow down thine ear, O Lord, hear me: for I am poor and needy. Preserve my soul; for I am holy..." By saying he was "holy" he meant "there is no sin in my life that might have caused my plight that I have not confessed." Not all sickness is caused by sin. Some is. Therefore, a person should confess any known sin in the event it is the cause. It is essential to removing the cause in order to achieve the intended end result.

Notice also that it is not the anointing with oil that is using the best medicine available that heals, but "...the prayer of faith shall save the sick." If anything will heal the sick it is prayer. Tim applied the truths taught in this text in the way intended. It was through prayer that God blessed with success the medical means employed.

How about Ralph? He and his loved ones were no less conscientious. This is one of the mysteries that must be understood in light of God's superior love and knowledge. His experience demonstrates that the James passage is not a "Passport to Planetary Perpetuation." Ralph was transferred to a higher command. God has not promised us perpetual life on planet Earth. He has provided for eternal life in His presence. This puts the Christian in a no-lose position.

Individual and collective prayer for the sick is expedient. In discounting literal anointing with oil, we must not devalue praying for the sick. When all that God requires is done, then you can be assured that whatever the result it is of the Lord. The outcome can then be responded to in the spirit of

I Thessalonians 5:16-18:
   "Rejoice evermore. Pray without ceasing.
   In everything give thanks."

9
FASTING AND PRAYER

Fasting and prayer are commended in Scripture. Both are encouraged but if you can only do one PRAY. When you do fast it should be done with a humble spirit. Don't brag about it or go around all glum as though sad about doing it. Just do it!

"Moreover, when you fast, do not be like the hypocrites, with a sad countenance. For they disfigure their faces that they may appear to men to be fasting. Assuredly, I say to you, they have their reward." (Matthew 6:16). Before starting to fast ask yourself if this is of the Lord for me to do? A second question, is my heart clean? Why am I doing it?

The prophet Isaiah reveals why God calls for fasting: "Is not this the fast I have chosen? To loose the bonds of wickedness, to undo the heavy burdens, to let the oppressed go free, and that you break every yoke" (Isaiah 58: 6). Fasting is not an attempt to bribe God. The question is not what will I get out of it but what does God want out of me. It is not to change God but to allow Him to change us. The reason for fasting is to focus on God, fill your mind with Him. In bringing your body into subjection to physical needs you should be reminded to bring all of your life into subjection to God. In this time of prayer don't try to be an advisor to God. Seek His will and submit to it. A good starting point is to commit to Him and ask Him to enable you to show forth the "fruit of the Spirit" in all of your life to all people. Study Galatians 5: 22, 23. Study this passage and conscientiously commit to each in daily affairs. Ask Him to work in your life making you a healer who shows compassion to all people. Ask Him to help you rid your life of guile and deception lest you be as the hypocrites who fasted without submission. Concentrate on getting your life right with God personally.

There are Bible examples of persons fasting as an expression of affliction and sorrow (I Samuel 31:13 & II Samuel 1:12). It evidenced repentance by some (I Kings 21:27). That is an admirable reason.

One reason for ancient Israel's dilemma was forced fasting when they should have been engaged in "joy and gladness and cheerful feasts" (Zechariah 8:19). Ask His forgiveness for straying from a fuller commitment to be His witnesses. Pray for the church to return to the goal of reaching, teaching, winning, and developing souls. Ask Him to work in the collective body of the church in order for it to be a more effective witness. Ask the Lord to deliver the church from living in the past and focus on a bright new day. There are various types of fasting. Don't consider you and your way better than that of anyone else. It is a personal and private affair. If you encounter anyone boasting about it you know such a person is not doing it for the right reason. It is not intended to impress people or twist God's arm.

Fasting in the Bible involved depriving oneself of food. If a person is inclined to deprive him or her self of any thing else that can be good but it is not Biblical fasting. It may very well be good to do but it is not what is meant by fasting in Scripture. One type of fasting involves ingesting only liquids for a period of time be it a day or 40 days. Some eat only one meal a day before sunrise or after sunset. Perhaps the most common time spent in a one day fast is to go from sundown to sundown. An effective fast involves abstaining from food for 24 hours. The length of the fast is a personal matter. Don't put more emphasis on fasting than on prayer. Intensify and increase the time spent in prayer during a fast. Spend more time reading Scripture and meditating on God's Word. For medical reasons persons with certain medical conditions should consult their doctor in advance. For persons not familiar with fasting you might experience light headaches, stomach emptiness, bad breath, and keen sense of smell. If so let these things be a physical call issued by your body to pray. The spiritual benefits of fasting far exceed the physical liabilities. Using the approach you feel pleases the Lord for you to employ make your time of fasting and prayer a time of submission to God and supplication.

AN ANCIENT BENEDICTION

"May the Lord Jesus Christ, who is the Splendor of the eternal Light, remove from your hearts the darkness of night. Amen.

May He drive far from you the snares of the crafty enemy, and ever set to guard you the Angel of light. Amen.

That you may rise to your morning praises, kept safe in Him, in whom consists all the fullness of your salvation. Amen.

May the Lord bless you, and protect you with His own Right Hand. Amen.

May He deliver you from all temptations of this life, and pour the grace of the Holy Spirit into your hearts. Amen.

May He take away from you every stain of sin, and lead you to the splendor of all His Saints. Amen.

May the Lord our God hear you, and favorably look on every one who calls to Him in need. Amen.

May He graciously grant the solace which human weakness needs, and avert the sins which oppose you. Amen.

And may He ever grant you all things profitable, both for your soul and bodies. Amen.

May the Almighty bless you from on high. Amen.

May He look upon your labor with favorable countenance, and hear your petitions with a pitying ear. Amen.

May he make your work well pleasing to Himself, and preserve your life in holiness and peace. Amen."